AUTHOR

Arturo Giusti, born on March 25, 2001, has been passionate about armored vehicles, logistic and improvised vehicles since childhood and entered the field of study only in 2018 by writing for the online magazine Tank Encyclopedia in which he has more than 80 articles to his credit, mainly focusing on Italian vehicles. He has recently started collaborating with the magazine Military History for which he published in December 2023 an article inherent in the evolution of the North Korean armored component up to 1990.

PUBLISHING'S NOTES

None of unpublished images or text of our book may be reproduced in any format without the expressed written permission of Luca Cristini Editore (already Soldiershop.com) when not indicate as marked with license creative commons 3.0 or 4.0. Luca Cristini Editore has made every reasonable effort to locate, contact and acknowledge rights holders and to correctly apply terms and conditions to Content.

Every effort has been made to trace the copyright of all the photographs. If there are unintentional omissions, please contact the publisher in writing at: info@soldiershop.com, who will correct all subsequent editions.

Our trademark: Luca Cristini Editore©, and the names of our series & brand: Soldiershop, Witness to war, Museum book, Bookmoon, Soldiers&Weapons, Battlefield, War in colour, Historical Biographies, Darwin's view, Fabula, Altrastoria, Italia Storica Ebook, Witness To History, Soldiers, Weapons & Uniforms, Storia etc. are herein © by Luca Cristini Editore.

LICENSES COMMONS

This book may utilize part of material marked with license creative commons 3.0 or 4.0 (CC BY 4.0), (CC BY-ND 4.0), (CC BY-SA 4.0) or (CC0 1.0). We give appropriate attribution credit and indicate if change were made in the acknowledgments field. Our WTW books series utilize only fonts licensed under the SIL Open Font License or other free use license.

For a complete list of Soldiershop titles please contact Luca Cristini Editore on our website: www.soldiershop.com or www.cristinieditore.com. E-mail: info@soldiershop.com

▲ Camionetta SPA-Viberti AS43 with waterproof structure

Title: **ARMOURED CARS OF THE ITALIAN SOCIAL REPUBLIC 1943 - 1945** Code.: **WTW-055 EN**
By Arturo Giusti
ISBN code: 9791255890676 first edition January 2024
Language: English; size: 177,8x254mm Cover & Art Design: Luca S. Cristini

WITNESS TO WAR (SOLDIERSHOP) is a trademark of Luca Cristini Editore, via Orio, 33D - 24050 Zanica (BG) ITALY.

WITNESS TO WAR

ARMOURED CARS OF THE ITALIAN SOCIAL REPUBLIC 1943 - 1945

PHOTOS & IMAGES FROM WORLD WARTIME ARCHIVES

ARTURO GIUSTI

BOOKS TO COLLECT

CONTENTS

A Brief History of Italian Armoured cars .... pag. 5

Service in the Italian Social Republic .... pag. 21

    Carrozzeria Speciale on SPA-Viberti AS43 .... pag. 23

    SPA-Viberti AS43 Autoprotected cars .... pag. 40

    SPA-Viberti AS43 Armoured cars .... pag. 51

    SPA-Viberti AS43 Armoured Ambulance .... pag. 57

    The Gruppo Arditi Camionettisti Italiani .... pag. 59

    The Police Armoured cars of Italian Africa .... pag. 73

    Transportkorps Speer and Luftwaffe .... pag. 81

    The Partisan Armoured cars .... pag. 83

Acknowledgements .... pag. 96

Bibliography .... pag. 97

▲ A Scotti-Isotta Fraschini 20/70 Model 1941 *Cannon-Mitragliera* displayed at the La Spezia Naval Technical Museum in 2020. The Scotti-Isotta Fraschini had the same characteristics as the Breda and fired the same ammunition, simplifying the logistics chain of the Royal Army. (Author)

A BRIEF HISTORY OF ITALIAN ARMOURED CARS

The iconic Italian desert Armoured cars were born out of the need of the *Libyan Sahara Command* to counter the British Long Range Desert Group[1] (LRDG) in early 1941.
The first armoured car models were simple FIAT-SPA AS37 desert Armoured cars[2] armed with Breda-SAFAT aircraft-sourced machine guns and *20/65 Model 1935 Breda 20/65 Model 1935 machine guns* loaded on the flatbeds[3] with the aim of intercepting LRDG patrols.
After the first clashes with British patrols in the Libyan desert, the *Regio Esercito* realised the need to develop vehicles for long-range reconnaissance and to counter British Armoured cars with similar vehicles, which the *Libyan Sahara Command* had been requesting for some time.
The High Command of the Royal Army planned to produce them to equip the 10th Arditi Regiment, which was created on 26 April 1942[4]. In December of the same year, it was also planned to adopt the armoured carettes from special units to be set up in the garrisons between Tunis and Tripoli. These units had the task of escorting columns, patrolling the areas assigned to them and defending the bases against incursions of Commonwealth troops from French Chad or Egypt. These units were equipped, among other vehicles, with 2 Armoured cars with 20/65 Model 1935 Breda 20/65 cannon-machine guns, 2 Armoured cars with 47/32 Model 1935 cannons and 4 with machine guns to provide adequate and heterogeneous suppressive fire and support in the event of a clash with the enemy[5].
The first project of such vehicles developed and produced in Italy was the *SPA-Viberti AS42 'Saharan' Desert Armoured car* built on the mechanics of the *Autoblinda AB41*[6].
The *SPA-Viberti AS42 'Sahariana' Desert Armoured car* retained the same chassis and engine as the armoured car.
In order to simplify production, lighten weight and reduce costs, the double steering was removed, which was superfluous on small Armoured cars, and steering was limited to the front wheels only, while retaining four-wheel drive.
The FIAT-SPA ABM 2 6-cylinder, in-line, 4,994 cm^3 petrol engine, delivering 88 hp, ensured a top speed of 84 km/h on the road, a more than adequate speed for a 6-tonne vehicle in combat order. The range, thanks to the 145-litre fuel tank, was 535 km on the road and about 350 km in varied terrain.

---

1 The unit specialised in long-range reconnaissance, intelligence gathering and desert navigation. Well armed and with well-trained soldiers, it was able to carry out very dangerous missions within the Axis lines.
2 The FIAT-SPA AS37 Saharan (AS) Armoured cars were light Armoured cars developed by FIAT in collaboration with the SPA on the chassis of the FIAT-SPA TL37 artillery tractor specifically for desert use.
3 R. H. Romain, *Il Sahara Italiano nella Seconda Guerra Mondiale*, Rome, Stato Maggiore dell'Esercito, Ufficio Storico, 2011, op. cit. in bibliography.
4 Still in two battalions at the time.
5 N. Pignato, F. Cappellano, *Gli Autoveicoli da Combattimento dell'Esercito Italiano (1940-1945), Tomo I, Volume Secondo*, Roma, USSME, 2002 pag. 446, op. cit. in bibliografia.
6 The *AB41 Autoblinda* was probably the most successful vehicle produced and employed by the *Regio Esercito* during the Second World War. Developed from the AB40, it was produced in 667 examples and used on all fronts of the war.

The characteristic body of the armoured car was developed and manufactured by Officine Viberti[7] in Turin. A total of twenty 20-litre petrol canisters were carried in four rows of five canisters on the sides of the vehicle[8] and guaranteed a total range of over 2,000 km, enabling the vehicles to carry out reconnaissance missions far beyond the Italian lines in Africa. Another two mounts on the front mudguards carried four canisters for drinking water[9].

For radio equipment, the SPA-Viberti AS42 'Saharan' desert Armoured cars were equipped with a TXO-OC3 transceiver station manufactured by the Anonymous Society John Geloso of Milan. This compact and reliable station had the advantage that it could be carried in a travel case and thus be easily transported on Armoured cars. This radio equipment, was developed from the German SE 92/3 station from which it differed in the valves, which were indirectly heated with 6.3 volt ignition. The TXO-OC3 transceiver station had a range of almost 200 km on direct waves. As the war continued, the RN5 radio station was also tested to be equipped on command vehicles, but due to delays and the Armistice of 8 September 1943, the Armoured cars were never equipped with this station.

The primary armament was housed in a universal stanchion mount in the centre of the chassis, which could be equipped with a 20/65 Model 1935 Breda 20/65 Model 1935 cannon-mirror gun with a useful range of about 2,500 metres against aerial targets and 5,000 metres against ground targets. The weapon was fed by 12-round clips and had a muzzle velocity of 840 m/s. The 47/32 Model 1935 cannon with a maximum range of 7,000 metres and a muzzle velocity of 630 m/s with armour-piercing projectiles could also be mounted on the carrier. Alternatively, the small Armoured cars could be armed with a Swiss-made Solothurn S-18/1000[10] 20 mm anti-tank gun with a range comparable to that of the Breda gun-machine gun and fed by removable 10-round magazines. A total of three medium machine gun[11] mounts could be mounted: two at the rear and one at the front on the driver's right. All weapons had a 360° field of fire, allowing the vehicle to open fire in any direction with several weapons at once. Despite the presence of the three mounts, it was not common practice to carry more than two weapons on board, probably due to the shortage of machine guns in the Italian ranks throughout the North African Campaign.

The ammunition reserve consisted of 1,200 20-mm rounds for the machine-gun and 350 47-mm rounds[12], however, no ammunition data is available for the Solothurn S-18/1000 and on-board machine guns.

---

7 Officine Viberti was a company specialising in the body-building of vehicles (mainly Armoured cars) and the production of trailers and tankers. The factory, with 1,517 workers and 263 employees in 1943, occupied an area of 70,000 m² in the block between Corso Peschiera, Corso Trapani, Corso Monte Cucco and Via Lorenzo Delleani.
8 In various sources, it is reported that crews carried additional canisters in the fighting compartment to increase the already very long range.
9 In pictures of the time, jerrycans for drinking water can be distinguished by their white-painted side ribs. Much rarer, however, were the jerrycans for transporting lubricating oil, with the ribs painted black.
10 The Solothurn S-18/1000 anti-tank rifle was acquired by the Royal Army beginning in 1940. In Italian service it was better known as the 'S' Carbine, and from 1942, as the 'S' Anti-tank Rifle.
11 The pictures suggest to us how the Breda Model 1937 Medium Machine Gun was the standard weapon, but there is no shortage of examples of *SPA-Viberti AS42 Desert Armoured cars* armed with Breda Model 1938 or Vickers K captured at the LRDG.
12 N. Pignato, F. Cappellano, *Gli Autoveicoli da Combattimento dell'Esercito Italiano (1940-1945), Tomo I, Volume Secondo*, Roma, USSME, 2002 p. 447-448, op. cit. in bibliography.

The prototype of the *SPA-Viberti AS42 Desert Armoured car was* presented on 9 July 1942 and after testing was not adopted until December 1942[13].

The success of the *SPA-Viberti AS42 'Saharan' Desert Armoured car* was unprecedented, the vehicle proved to be suitable for combat against British troops, being able, thanks to its autonomy, to pursue British reconnaissance and sabotage units that were sighted, and in turn carry out infiltration missions behind enemy lines.

The total production of the vehicle is very uncertain, military sources report an order for 120 units, but the total number produced and delivered is unknown[14].

Unfortunately, excellence always comes at a very high cost, and the AS42 was no exception. What's more, for every *SPA-Viberti AS42 Desert Armoured car* that was produced, a chassis was taken off the assembly line, reducing the production of the equally valuable *AB41 Autoblinde*.

FIAT and SPA then began to develop a vehicle based on a prototype developed by the *Libyan Sahara Command*, on the chassis of the FIAT-SPA AS37 desert armoured car[15]. The vehicle would have been cheaper than the AS42 and would not have affected the production of armoured cars. The project began in October 1942, the chassis of the AS37 was lowered[16] and reinforced, the engine was modified and, of course, the bodywork was changed, again produced by Officine Viberti.

The new vehicle was presented in January 1943, renamed the *SPA-Viberti AS43 Desert Armoured car* and tested.

The armament consisted of a *47/32 Model 1935* or *20/65 Model 1935 Breda cannon-machine gun mounted on a* 360° mount in the centre of the rear platform and a *Breda Model 1937 medium machine gun* on a gooseneck mount in front, operated by the commander.

Before mass production of the new armoured car began, however, the North African Campaign was in its dramatic final stages and in order not to lose the order, the Armoured cars were modified for use in the motherland[17] in agreement with the *Regio Esercito*, losing the term 'Desertica' and becoming the *SPA-Viberti AS43 Armoured caretta*.

The new vehicle was powered by a petrol engine, SPA 18VT 4ª Variant, in-line, four-cylinder, water-cooled, four-stroke, delivering a maximum power of 75 hp at 2,000 rpm. The engine was an improved version of the SPA Type 18TL mounted on the TL37 artillery tractor and its variants. The gearbox had five gears plus reverse and a maximum speed of 68.5 km/h. The range was 750 km thanks to 240 litres of fuel in two unprotected side tanks. Thanks to the 6 transportable tanks[18] the maximum range was up to 1,120 km.

---

13 N. Pignato, F. Cappellano, *Gli Autoveicoli da Combattimento dell'Esercito Italiano (1940-1945), Tomo I, Volume Secondo*, Roma, USSME, 2002 p. 448, op. cit. in bibliography.

14 E. Finazzer and L. Carretta, *Le Camionette del Regio Esercito*, Trento, Gruppo Modellistico Trentino, 2014, p. 18, reports the registration of a total of *'some eighty'* AS42s and that the November 1942 bombing destroyed *'several dozen small Armoured cars'* before registration.

15 In the late summer of 1942, the *Libyan Sahara Command* presented the Centro Studi ed Esperienze della Motorizzazione with an example of a FIAT-SPA AS37 Saharan armoured car converted into a lorry. N. Pignato, F. Cappellano, *Gli Autoveicoli da Combattimento dell'Esercito Italiano (1940-1945), Tomo I, Volume Secondo*, Roma, USSME, 2002 p. 452, op. cit. in bibliography.

16 The clearance increased from 390 mm to 345 mm. E. Finazzer and L. Carretta, *Le Camionette del Regio Esercito*, Trento, Gruppo Modellistico Trentino, 2014, p. 18, op. cit. in bibliography.

17 Compared to the original design, the steering components in the rear axle were removed and the bodywork simplified by removing two side racks for five canisters each, which were replaced with two ammunition lockers.

18 On the mudguards there were 2 rear and 2 front single supports.

The ammunition reserve consisted of 960 rounds of 20 mm ammunition in 80 plates: 36 in four racks arranged on the bottom of the rear platform while the remaining 48 were divided between the two side lockers. Alternatively, the 47 mm cannon had a reserve of 160 rounds, 60 in the racks on the platform and 50 in each side locker. For secondary armament, there were 100 20-round plates placed in a rack between the commander and driver and in two racks above the side lockers[19].

The new order of 12 August 1943[20] stipulated that the SPA-Viberti AS43 and SPA-Viberti AS42 'Underground'[21] Armoured cars were to be deployed in the new amphibious anti-landing and anti-parachute roles.

As with the AS43s, the SPA-Viberti AS42 'Saharan' desert Armoured cars were modified for continental use. Modifications included the removal of a row of canisters on each side of the body, replacing them with a huge metal box to store ammunition from the main armament. This modification was made because in the homeland the Armoured cars did not need to operate hundreds of kilometres from their home bases. The 'Metropolitan' model is also sometimes called the 'Saharan II' or 'Type II'.

Some 'Saharan' AS42s that did not make it in time to be sent to North Africa were employed in the new roles assigned in Sicily with modest results. A total of 180 SPA-Viberti AS43 camionettes were ordered, but only 23 were produced before the Armistice, of which eight were delivered to the Depot of the 1st Carrista Infantry Regiment in Vercelli between 28 and 29 July 1943[22], seven to the Depot of the 4th Carrista Infantry Regiment in Rome on 4 August 1943[23] and the last eight to the Depot of the 33rd Carrista Infantry Regiment in Parma in two lots on 4 and 14 August 1943.

Officine Viberti confirmed a total production of 167 or 169 plus 13 examples produced to German specifications[24]. The last examples were delivered to the State Police by Officine Viberti in two separate batches in January 1946[25].

The last and lesser-known armoured car model was the Desert Armoured car Model 1943, which, however, was only desert in name and not in use. This armoured car model was developed and modified by the Centro Studi ed Esperienze della Motorizzazione in Rome

---

19 R. A. Riccio, *Italian Tanks and Combat Vehicles of World War II*, Mattioli, 2010 p. 252, op. cit. in bibliography.
20 Circolare Tipo: 'Documento n.5500/A', oggetto: *Concetti Fondamentali ai quali deve essere Informato l'Impiego delle Compagnie Camionette ed il loro Addestramento*, drafted by General of the Army Corps and Inspector of Motorised and Armoured Troops Augusto de Pignier, taken from N. Pignato, F. Cappellano, *Gli Autoveicoli da Combattimento dell'Esercito Italiano, Tomo II Volume II*, Roma, USSME, 2002, pages 889 - 891, op. cit. in bibliography.
21 As with the AS43s, the AS42 'Saharan' was modified for continental use. Modifications included the removal of a row of canisters on each side of the bodywork, replacing them with a huge metal box for storing ammunition.
22 It was planned in Vercelli, the creation of the *1ª Compagnia Camionette da 20 mm* to be set up by 10 June 1943. Document No. 40', *Costruzione di una Compagnia Camionette*, taken from N. Pignato, F. Cappellano, *Gli Autoveicoli da Combattimento dell'Esercito Italiano (1940-1945), Tomo II, Volume Secondo*, Roma, USSME, 2002, p. 886, op. cit. in bibliography.
23 The *2ª Compagnia Camionette da 20 mm* was present in Rome at the date of the Armistice. We can therefore assume that the Parma company was called *3ª Compagnia Camionette da 20 mm*.
24 E. Finazzer and L. Carretta, *Le Camionette del Regio Esercito*, Trento, Gruppo Modellistico Trentino, 2014, p. 21, op. cit. in bibliography.
25 N. Pignato, F. Cappellano, *Gli Autoveicoli da Combattimento dell'Esercito Italiano, Tomo II Volume II*, Rome, USSME, 2002, p. 455, op. cit. in bibliography.

to equip the Battaglione d'Assalto Motorizzato26 and produced in a very limited number of examples in early 1943. For production, the Centro Studi ed Esperienze della Motorizzazione proceeded by modifying some FIAT-SPA AS37s by removing part of the cockpit, doors and windscreen. The vehicle had as main armament a Breda 20/65 Model 1935 cannon-machine gun, and as secondary armament a Breda Model 1937 medium machine gun operated by the commander. From the few photos found of the vehicle, the machine gun had an anti-aircraft reticle sight and a metal stock to dampen recoil. The sight and stock were the normal equipment of the machine gun and it seems that these Armoured cars were the only ones to have used them in service.

---

26 The *Motorised Assault Battalion* arose from the disbandment of the *'Red Arrows' Regiment*. Before the Armistice, it had 24 *SPA-Viberti AS42 'Underground'* and 11 *Desert Armoured cars Model 1943 in* service.

▲ *SPA-Viberti AS43 Armoured cars* ready for delivery to the departments. One can clearly see the three-tone camouflage and the absence of armament and number plates. The second vehicle in the row is equipped with *Pirelli Type 'Artiglio' tyres* while the other three vehicles are fitted with *Pirelli Type 'Green Seal'* tyres. (Courtesy of Daniele Guglielmi via Enrico Finazzer)

▲ Front view of a *SPA-Viberti AS42 'Saharan' desert armoured car* with windscreen covered by a waterproof tarpaulin. The vehicle is ready for delivery, obviously unarmed and without a tripod for the machine gun. (Courtesy of Claudio Pergher via Enrico Finazzer)

▼ The same vehicle seen from the rear and without a windscreen cover. The number plates, like the armament, were also added after delivery to the army. The vehicle is fitted with *Pirelli 'Raiflex'* tyres. (Courtesy of Claudio Pergher via Enrico Finazzer)

▲ Another shot of the *SPA-Viberti AS42 'Sahariana' Desert Armoured car* covered by the waterproof tarpaulin. The side parts of the tarpaulin are missing. The pictures in the series were taken inside the Officine Viberti facilities in Turin, as can also be seen by the presence of trailers ready for delivery. (Courtesy of Claudio Pergher via Enrico Finazzer)

▼ A *SPA-Viberti AS42 'Metropolitana' armoured car* completely covered in camouflage and equipped with *Pirelli 'Artiglio'* type tyres. The ammunition box on the side is the easiest way to distinguish the two armoured car models. (Courtesy of Claudio Pergher via Enrico Finazzer)

▲ Interior of the *SPA-Viberti AS42 'Saharan' Desert Armoured car* without armament and with lowered windscreen. The flame-cutter plate between the engine compartment and the fighting compartment is removed, making the cooling water and lubricating oil tanks visible (unchanged from the AB armoured cars). (Courtesy of Claudio Pergher via Enrico Finazzer)

▼ Another picture of the same Armoured cars ready for delivery. Note the shield with bulletproof glass for the driver and the starting handle on the armoured car guard. Both images were taken inside the SPA factory in Turin. (Courtesy of Daniele Guglielmi via Enrico Finazzer)

▲ *Autoblinda AB41* advances in the Libyan Desert during the North African Campaign. The *autoblinda* and the *SPA-Viberti AS42 Armoured cars* shared the same chassis. In this magnificent image, note the SPA-logoed hubcap and Pirelli stamping on the shoulder of the Type 'Libya' tire. (Central State Archives)

▼ Another image of *Autoblinda AB41* plowing through the Marmarico Dunes sea during the North African Campaign. The vehicle belonged to the 3rd Armored Group *'Nizza'* which operated in the ranks of the 132nd Armored Division *'Ariete'*. Summer 1942. (Central State Archives)

▲ One of the small Armoured cars made by the Libyan Sahara Command during the West African Campaign. This is a *FIAT-SPA AS37 armoured car* converted into a desert armoured carette by removing some body parts and adopting a Model 1935 47/32 Cannon in the cargo bed. Behind the improvised armoured carette, two *SPA-Viberti AS42 'Saharan' Desert Armoured cars* are noted. (USSME)

▼ A Breda 20/65 Model 1935 *Cannon-Mitragliera* positioned on a Hellenic mountain during the Greek Campaign. (Central State Archives)

▲ Italian artillerymen probably posing for the Istituto Luce crew operate a Breda 20/65 Model 1935 *Cannon-Mitragliera*. Greek Front, Winter 1941. (Central State Archives)

▼ A servant positions a 12-round plate for another Breda 20/65 Model 1935 *Cannon-Mitragliera* in Greece. Again the gunners are posed, as we can see from the presence of the tie worn by both soldiers. (Central State Archives)

▲ A 1935 Model 47/32 Cannon is operated by a crew of Alpines during the Russian Campaign. Although it proved effective during the Spanish War, the 47mm cannon demonstrated all its limitations in anti-tank fighting during World War II, but remained a good infantry support weapon. (Central State Archives)

▼ The crew of a 47/32 Cannon waits for the right moment to open fire at Soviet troops on the banks of the Dnepr River in Ukraine in the Fall of 1941.

▲ A Model 1935 47/32 Cannon in a well-camouflaged position during a training in anti-tank fighting in the summer of 1942. (Central State Archives)

▼ The crew of a *SPA-Viberti AS42 'Saharan' Desert Armoured car* is pictured during a break in the fighting. Two very unusual things can be seen in the image. The first is certainly the front Breda Model 1938 Medium Machine Gun, lacking an upper magazine. The second is the lubricating oil canister placed in the bottom row of the vehicle with the ribs painted black. Also interesting is the use of the windshield to "rest" the barrel of the anti-tank gun.

▲ Two bersaglieri place a Solothurn S-18-1000 anti-tank gun on its carriage for towing. Although the weapon proved effective against the sensitive points of several British armored vehicles, it was very heavy to carry. (Central State Archives)

▲ A group of Bersaglieri open fire at Soviet troops during the Russian Campaign well under cover behind a dry stone wall. The weapon they are using is a Breda Model 1937 Medium Machine Gun. (Central State Archives)

▲ A propaganda photo showing some Italian machine gunners inside a makeshift fort in Montenegro in the winter of 1942. Note the 20-round plates for the Breda Model 1937 machine gun. (Central State Archives)

▼ A Bersagliere from the *8th Autonomous Armored Bersaglieri Battalion* filmed while servicing a Breda Model 1938 Medium Machine Gun on the turret of an AB41 Autoblinda. Although very rare, the weapon was employed on small Armoured cars. (Central State Archives)

SERVICE IN THE ITALIAN SOCIAL REPUBLIC

After the Armistice of Cassibile on 8 September 1943, the first unit to deploy the Armoured cars were the MVSN soldiers who did not accept the surrender and gathered at the *'Mussolini' Barracks* in Rome's Viale Romania.

These soldiers, who chose to continue fighting alongside the Germans, were part of various units of the disbanded *1ª Legionary Armoured Division 'M'*, which had surrendered its arms to the Germans on 12 September 1943 and joined them on 16 September[27].

From the following day, at the behest of Consul General Renzo Montagna[28], the new headquarters of the Republican Fascist Party was opened in the historic Palazzo Wedekind in Piazza Colonna. The soldiers gathered at the *Caserma 'Mussolini'* were then assigned to guard the building with the help of two M13/40 tanks taken from the depot of the *4th Carrista Infantry Regiment* abandoned after the armistice[29]. At least one *Desert Armoured car Model 1943* was found in the depot and deployed.

The armoured car had been deployed during the Defence of Rome between 9 and 10 September and was unarmed (probably sabotaged by the Camionettisti). The vehicle was almost certainly only used to transport the garrison from the barracks to the Wedekind Palace on a daily basis and to patrol the streets of Rome.

When the militiamen left for Montichiari to form the future *Armoured Group M 'Leonessa'* on 29 September 1943, it is very likely that the armoured car remained in Rome[30] as, in the period following the Second World War, at least one example was in service with the *I° Reparto Celere 'Lazio'* of the *Polizia di Stato*[31] in Rome.

---

27 S. Corbatti and M. Nava,...*Like Diamond! I Carristi Italiani 1943-'45*, Brussels Laran Edition, 2008, p. 128.
28 Renzo Montagna, who was liberated by the Germans on 8 September, took command of the MVSN in the capital by settling in the *'Mussolini' Barracks* and remained in command until 18 September, when Alessandro Pavolini arrived in the capital.
29 P. Crippa, *I Carristi di Mussolini, Il Gruppo Corazzato "Leonessa" dalla MVSN alla RSI*, Witness to War, May 2019, p. 17.
30 The theory is confirmed by the absence of *Model 1943 Desert Armoured cars* in service with *Armoured Group M 'Leonessa'*.
31 The vehicle was photographed during a parade by the *Mobile Blindists* of the *1st Celere Department of* the *State Police* in 1947.

▲ A *SPA-Viberti AS42 'Metropolitan' Armoured car* of the Motorised Assault Battalion armed with a Model 1935 47/32 Cannon and a Model 1937 Breda Medium Machine Gun. The picture was taken in Rome in the convulsive days following the armistice. (Nino Arena)

▼ An interesting picture taken in September 1943 showing a 3rd Series M13/40 Tank and a *Desert Armoured car Model 1943* used by soldiers of the disbanded 1st Armoured Legionary Division 'M' to guard Palazzo Wedekind, headquarters of the new Republican Fascist Party. The vehicles are located between Piazza Colonna and Piazza di Monte Citorio. (Courtesy of Paolo Crippa)

Carrozzeria Speciale on SPA-Viberti AS43

The *Carrozzeria Speciale on SPA-Viberti AS43*[32] was the only vehicle produced and used by the *Republican National Guard*[33] to be developed and actually mass-produced, albeit in limited numbers and used by the *Armoured Group M 'Leonessa'* of the *Republican National Guard*.

The total number of vehicles produced is not certain: according to a publication by some veterans of the *Armoured Group M 'Leonessa'*, there were a total of 10 so-called *'Zerbino' type armoured cars*. In more recent publications[34] however, it was clarified thanks to the testimony of Lance Corporal Bartuli[35], a veteran of the group, that the nickname *'Zerbino'* was given to many improvised vehicles of the armoured group.

In more current publications, the number of special bodies has been reduced[36] to a more plausible 2-6.

Another source that seems to confirm the more meagre production is a Report of the *Turin Army Arsenal*[37] drawn up on 23 March 1945 in which, the arsenal lists the equipment supplied to the Turin branch of the GNR. Together with some artillery pieces, *'Number Four armoured and self-protected vehicles' were supplied,* although no mention is made of which particular self-protected vehicle this was.

The project was initiated by Officine Viberti[38] after a probable request by Prefect Zerbino[39] for the production of armoured vehicles.

The original plans for the vehicle are dated 18 January 1944, when development of the armoured structure for the *SPA-Viberti AS43 Armoured carettes* began. The last modification to the design is dated 3 April 1944, indicating how quick and simple the development of this interesting vehicle was.

As mentioned, the armour plates were produced by the *Turin Army Arsenal*, which sent them to Officina Viberti, which was responsible for coachbuilding the chassis produced at SPA.

For production, the armoured car chassis were stripped of their bodywork[40], the armour plates were bolted to an internal skeleton as was the case with most Italian armoured vehicles of the time. The total weight of the armour plates was 911 kg excluding, of course, the

---

32 Also often referred to as *'Autoblinda AS43'* or *'Tipo Zerbino'*. The second designation is due to Paolo Zerbino, Head of the Province of Turin from 21 October 1943 to 7 May 1944, who ordered the production of emergency vehicles for the fascist forces.
33 The *Republican National Guard* was the force with internal police and military tasks that emerged after the armistice of 8 September from the ashes of the MVSN.
34 S. Corbatti and M. Nava,...*Like Diamond! I Carristi Italiani 1943-'45*, Brussels Laran Edition, 2008, p. 142.
35 Lance Corporal G. Bartuli was a driver of vehicles of the Armoured Group M 'Leonessa'.
36 P. Crippa, *Storia dei Reparti Corazzati della Repubblica Sociale Italiana,* Milan, Marcia Edizioni, October 2022, p. 146, op. cit. in bibliography.
37 Relazione Sull'*Arsenale Esercito di Torino* kept at AUSSME I1, Busta 36. It is interesting to note that after the Armistice the *Arsenale Regio Esercito di Torino* lost its 'Regio'.
38 The vehicle was inspired by the *Autoblinda AS37* (often referred to by various names such as 'Autoblindo TL37' or 'Autoblindo AS') developed by Ansaldo in 1941 for specific use in North Africa.
39 No precise data is available, but given the nickname of the vehicle, it is assumed by various sources that the Prefect of Turin financed the construction or arranged for the vehicles to be assigned to the *Armoured Group M 'Leonessa'*.
40 Unfortunately, we have no information about the chassis; the special bodies could have been produced from new chassis or on previously bodied Armoured cars.

steel skeleton and fasteners[41]. Unfortunately, it is impossible to give a precise estimate of the total weight of the vehicle, with about one and a half tonnes for the armoured superstructure and turret, the armament, ammunition and the weight of the bare chassis, which was 2,620 kg dry. The total was most likely around 6 tonnes in combat trim, not far off the total weight of the fully loaded armoured car.

The thickness of the plates is not indicated by official sources but it is plausible that it was around 8 mm, enough to protect the vehicle from enemy small arms fire. The turret armour was 18 mm at the front and 10 mm at the sides and rear.

At the front was the petrol engine, which had several cooling grilles at the front and two inspection hatches at the top for maintenance. The maximum speed of the armoured car was about 50 km/h while the range, thanks to the 120-litre tank mounted at the rear of the fighting chamber, was about 350 km.

Behind the engine compartment were the driver, on the right, and the captain, on the left. Both had the same seats used on the AB41, with a pivoting backrest, to allow easy entry and exit from the vehicle. For observation, both had front slits but no side slits.

Behind them sat the gunner on a folding seat mounted, with a tubular support, to the turret. The turret, mounted on the armoured structure, was the well-known *Model 1941 turret* used on *L6/40 Tanks*. It has often been assumed that the turrets came from *AB41 Autoblinde*, but the absence of a rear counterweight confirms that these turrets were taken from the SPA factories (where the *L6/40 Tanks* were produced) or salvaged from damaged crawlers.

Octagonal in shape, the turret had two hatches, an upper one to allow the gunner to observe the battlefield or for a quick escape. The second hatch, at the rear, had the sole purpose of facilitating the removal of the 20 mm cannon for maintenance by 'slipping' it from its mount. To open fire, the commander was equipped with two pedals mounted on a tubular stand connected to the cannon and machine gun via Bowden cables[42].

For the inside view, the gunner had, of course, a rifle scope coaxial to the cannon mounted on the left, a panoramic periscope (both manufactured by Officine San Giorgio) mounted on the turret ceiling on the right, and two loopholes on the sides. The loopholes, of the 'revolver' type, could be used to control the battlefield and for close-range defence by firing the gun provided.

The armament consisted of a *Breda 20/65 Model 1935* 20 mm *cannon-machine gun* and, coaxially on the right, a *Model 1938* 8 x 59 mm RB Breda medium machine gun, a vehicle version of the *Breda Model 1937 medium machine gun* with a 24-round upper two-piece magazine.

Under the turret were the access doors to the vehicle, which were divided into two parts and opened at the front.

From the few pictures found, it can be confirmed that the back of the combat chamber was occupied by the wooden racks for the magazines of the 20 mm cannon and at the bottom, for the 8 mm machine gun.

---

41 911.23 kg excluding the 642 items of hardware, hinges, hooks, steel skeleton.
42 Bowden cables are metal cables covered with a rubber sheath, the same cables used in bicycle brakes and gearboxes.

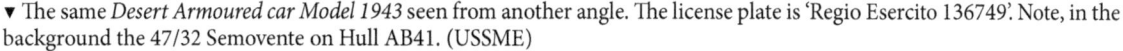

▲ The *Model 1943 Desert Armoured car* in the courtyard of the Rome DMV Study and Experience Center. The armament consists of a Model 1937 Medium Machine Gun equipped with an antiaircraft sight and metal stock in front and a 20/65 Model 1935 Breda Cannon-Mitra-gun. (USSME)

▼ The same *Desert Armoured car Model 1943* seen from another angle. The license plate is 'Regio Esercito 136749'. Note, in the background the 47/32 Semovente on Hull AB41. (USSME)

▲ The same enlarged image better shows us the *Model 1943 Desert Armoured car* without armament and equipped with Pirelli Type 'Green Seal' tires behind a 3rd Series M13/40 Tank parked to the side of Wedekind Palace. (Courtesy of Paolo Crippa)

In total there were 50 plates per cannon, equivalent to 400 rounds[43] and 60 magazines for the machine gun, equivalent to 1,440 rounds. A respectable reserve for a vehicle of this size, in fact, the *Autoblinda AB41, to give an* example, had a reserve of 456 20 mm and 1,992 8 mm rounds.

Behind the racks, protected by a flameproof bulkhead, was the triangular-shaped tank on which the spare wheel was placed, protected by the vehicle's sloping rear armour plate. The rear armour plate could be opened at the bottom to retrieve the spare wheel, and on its outer surface were the classic hoe tools: pick, shovel and hoist.

The wheels had 24"(60 cm) rims, which is the same diameter as the AB series armoured cars and the TL37 and TM40 artillery tractors. The front wheels were equipped with independent coil spring suspension coupled with hydraulic shock absorbers. The rear wheels were equipped with inverted leaf spring suspensions. The tyres adopted were Pirelli 'Artiglio' type[44] 9 x 24"(22.8 x 60 cm) for continental climates.

The armoured cars were not equipped with two-way radio systems, no small handicap for a vehicle of this type, which was often used on patrol missions where the use of radios could be crucial for requesting command support.

---

43 8-round plates were used on armoured vehicles instead of the classic 12-round plates used on Armoured cars or field guns due to lack of space in the turret.

44 The Armoured cars could be equipped with Pirelli Type 'Libia' 9.75 x 24"(25 x 60 cm), 'Libia Reinforced' and 'Green Seal' for use in desert terrain, and Pirelli Type 'Artiglio', 'Artiglio a Sezione Maggiorata' 11.25 x 24"(28.5 x 60 cm) and 'Raiflex' for continental terrain. Due to the political situation in the CSR, it could happen to see vehicles with tyres for desert terrain.

We do not have the date of the arrival of the Armoured cars at the *National Republican Guard* unit[45] nor a precise location of the Armoured cars within the unit as sources are conflicting. From the images that have come down to the present day, we can state that the Armoured cars were stationed at the *'Alessandro La Marmora' Barracks*[46] in Via Asti 22, the headquarters of the *1ª Compagnia Arditi Autocarrata*[47] of the *'Leonessa'* as early as March 1944, the month in which the unit moved from Montichiari to Turin.

At least in an early period the improvised armoured cars were painted in light Saharan khaki with the *'Leonessa'* symbols[48] painted on the front mudguards, sides and rear hatch of the turret.

Unfortunately, we do not have much data on the service of the special bodies in the anti-partisan struggle in Piedmont, as most official sources rarely mentioned the vehicles used in the actions or merely used generic terms such as 'Autoblinda' or 'Autoprotetta'.

Thanks to its integral protection and heavy armament, we can assume it was an adequate means to counter partisan gangs, which in most cases were without anti-tank weapons[49] and could in no way deal with such a vehicle.

On 23 March 1945, the *M Armoured Group 'Leonessa' paraded through* Turin for the last time and in the parade, only one *Special Body on SPA-Viberti AS43* paraded through the city streets. The presence of only one vehicle did not necessarily mean that the others were lost; the day before, in fact, units of the *'Leonessa'* left Turin were deployed in an anti-Partisan action in Valsesia. At least one armoured car was employed in this operation, but the model is not known.

By that time, the Turin-based department's vehicles had received a new three-tone camouflage with dark green and reddish-brown patches over the original light Saharan khaki camouflage used in the department's early months, very similar to the 'Continental' camouflage scheme adopted by the *Regio Esercito a* few months before the Armistice.

Speaking of camouflage, it seems only fair to point out that there are pictures of the Carrozzeria Speciale at Officine Viberti[50] with a three-tone camouflage that the armoured group did not adopt until December 1944[51].

It seems highly unlikely that the Turin-based company delivered the first two vehicles in April 1944 to the *'Leonessa'* in three-tone camouflage, which was almost immediately covered by the militia in monochrome camouflage, only to be repainted in the same camouflage scheme a few months later.

---

45 The first public appearance of two *Special Troops on SPA-Viberti AS43s* was on 23 April 1944, when they paraded, together with other department vehicles, in Turin.
46 The barracks were also home to two Public Order companies of the GNR and the Turin *Railway Militia Legion*. However, the barracks are also infamous for being the headquarters of the *Ufficio Politico Investigativo* (UPI) where partisans were interrogated and tortured.
47 Later renamed *1ª Compagnia Carri 'Aristide Lissa'* after Captain Aristide Lissa, company commander, who died in a clash with partisans on 7 June 1944 in Santino di San Bernardino, in the province of Novara.
48 The acronym GNR in black paint with a red 'm' intersected by a fascio littorio.
49 Between August 1944 and February 1945, 326 anti-tank weapons including Bazookas, PIATs and 70 anti-tank rifles were parachuted into Italian partisans. A very small number if one considers that in Piedmont alone there were about 50,000 partisans in April 1945. Technical Memorandum ORO-T-269, *Allied Supplies for Italian Partisans During World War II*, Washington DC, Department of the Army, Office of the Deputy Chief of Staff for Plans and Research, 4 February 1955, p. 36 op. cit. in bibliography.
50 The date when the pictures were taken is unknown, but the vehicles lacked the armament, which was fitted after delivery by Officine Viberti.
51 P. Crippa, *Storia dei Reparti Corazzati della Repubblica Sociale Italiana,* Milan, Marcia Edizioni, October 2022, p. 201, op. cit. in bibliography.

The vehicles photographed, unarmed, at Officine Viberti were probably produced after the delivery of a first batch of special bodies at the end of May, beginning of April 1944[52], thus confirming the possibility that more than two vehicles were actually produced and delivered, some of them already in three-tone camouflage.

At the end of April 1945, a detachment of the group, consisting of an *L6/40 Tank* and two armoured cars, one of which was definitely a *Special Carriage on SPA-Viberti AS43*[53], was sent to Valtellina in Lombardy, with the task of keeping the area clear of partisans. Valtellina was the area chosen by the Secretary of the National Fascist Party, Alessandro Pavolini, for the 'Ridotto Alpino Repubblicano', an area where the fascist units loyal to Mussolini fleeing from the cities of northern Italy could be massed and where they could resist the allied troops while Benito Mussolini fled to Switzerland. Together with the 'Leonessa' detachment, the 'Pesaro' Company of the *M Battalion 'Guardia del Duce'*, the units of the *XXXIX^a Black Brigade 'Raffaele Manganiello'* of Siena[54], the *XV^a Black Brigade 'Sergio Gatti'* of Sondrio, the *Autonomous Black Brigade 'Giovanni Gentile'*[55] and other GNR and *National Republican Army* units were present in Valtellina.

The 'Leonessa' detachment was located in Tirano, near Sondrio, a few kilometres from Switzerland. On the morning of 27 April, a column composed of the detachment of *Armoured Group M 'Leonessa'*, the 2nd *Battalion* of the *III^a Legion* of the *National Republican Frontier Guard 'Vetta d'Italia'*, by the *XXXVIIIth Black Brigade 'Ruy Blas Biagi'* from Pistoia and members of the *Milice française*[56] of the French Republic of Vichy, for a total of about 1,000 men under the command of GNR Frontier Major Renato Vanna, left for Sondrio to join Benito Mussolini. The column was immediately blocked on its way out of the city by partisan troops, triggering the Battle of Tirano.

On the night of 26 April, the *Partisan Brigade 'Gufi'* surrounded the town of Tirano. In the following hours, groups of partisans also arrived from the Val Grosina and the Sondalo area.

According to the accounts of a partisan veteran[57] there were about 300 partisans, without heavy weapons, apart from a few mortars that besieged the fascist forces.

On the morning of 27 April, the fascist column with the *L6/40 Tank* in the lead tried to reach Sondrio but was blocked at the Tirano exit by partisans.

Some soldiers, covered behind the silhouettes of armoured vehicles, tried to reach the Sanctuary of the Madonna outside Tirano, to try and make the partisan troops retreat, but without success. The fascists then returned to the town, barricading themselves in the 'Luigi Torelli' barracks

---

52 Another possible hypothesis is that the vehicles were repainted after a general overhaul at Officine Viberti. Here, too, it seems highly improbable since the symbols of the *M 'Leonessa' armoured group* are absent from the Officine Viberti pictures.
53 The second model of the armoured car is unknown but we can assume it was a second *Carrozzeria Speciale on SPA-Viberti AS43*.
54 Reported by ...*Like Diamond! I Carristi Italiani 1943-'45*, Brussels Laran Edition, 2008, p. 190, op. cit. in bibliography. It seems instead that the 'Raffaele Manganiello' was the XLI^a Florence *Black Brigade*.
55 At the time reduced to one company and renamed the *company 'Cremona'*.
56 The Milice *française* (French Militia) created to fight the Maquis of the French Resistance was placed in Tirano from 13 April 1945 under the command of Consul General Onorio Onori. The French unit was under the command of Captain Carus.
57 W. Marconi, *L'Aprile 1945 fra Tirano e Grosio*, Tirano, Museo Etnografico Tiranese, 1996, op. cit. in bibliography.

until the evening of 28 April when hostilities finally ceased with a total of 19 dead[58] in the fascist ranks and 2 in the partisan ranks. Mag. Vanna with 250 men tried to reach Lake Como on foot at night, but when the news of Mussolini's death arrived, he gave himself up to the partisans who took him and his men back to the *'Luigi Torelli' Barracks*, which had been converted into a prison after the surrender of the garrison. Major Vanna and 25 other officers and non-commissioned officers were later shot by the partisans.

After the surrender of the regular troops on 28 April, at least one *Special Body on SPA-Viberti AS43* was re-used by the partisan forces, as were at least two Peugeot 202 vans captured from the French[59]. Until 2 May 1945, the vehicles were used to patrol the area of the Mortirolo Pass, at 1,852 metres above sea level, where an attack by the *Iª Assault Legion M 'Tagliamento'* deployed in Alta Valcamonica was feared.

Unfortunately, traces of this vehicle are lost, just like the other special bodies that were probably destroyed during the clashes in Turin or sabotaged by the crews before the escape to Valtellina, which however stopped at Strambino Romano, 45 km north-west of Turin.

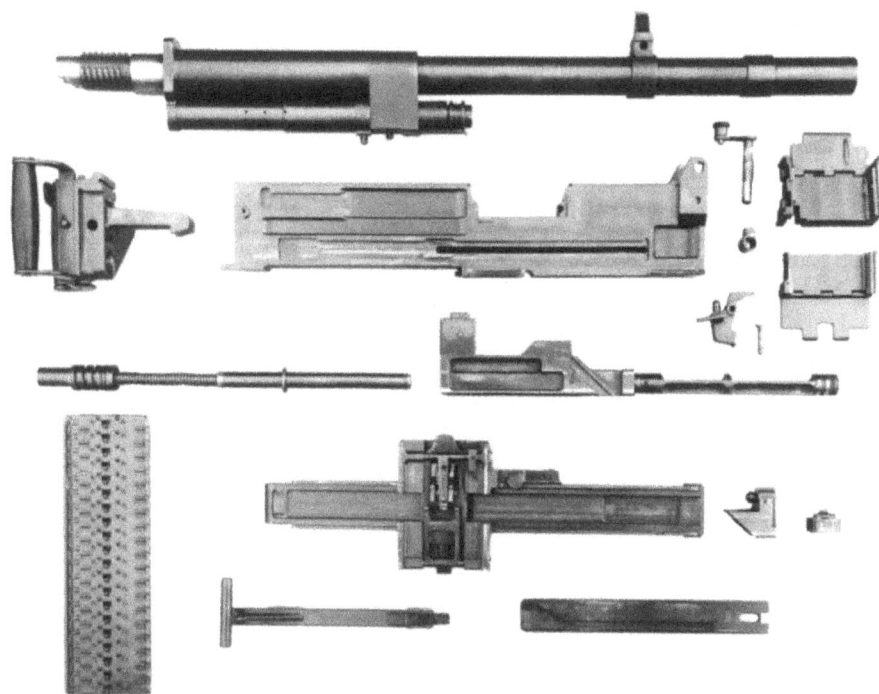

▲ Knolling of the mitragliatrice Breda Mod.1937. Usually weapon used on the Italian Armoured cars.

---

58 In detail: 9 GNR soldiers and black shirts, 2 auxiliaries, 5 French and 3 Germans.
59 Unfortunately, the sources do not mention how many vehicles were damaged or destroyed in the battle and how many were re-used by the partisans. The armoured car and vans appear in a picture after the battle in Partisan hands and are the only ones we can confirm were used.

▲ After the Tirano clashes, the *Carrozzeria Speciale on SPA-Viberti AS43* of the Armoured Group M 'Leonessa' was reused by local partisans. The picture was taken in Sondrio, with the armoured car at the head of a column of Peugeot 202 vans captured from the Milice française fighting alongside Italian Social Republic soldiers. (g.c. Tiranese Ethnographic Museum).

▲ ▼ Two magnificent pictures of the *AS37 Autoblinda* in service with General Gastone Gambara's Army Maneuver Corps Exploring Regiment at Sidi Rezegh in November 1941. The small prototype Autoblinda operated together with four *AB41 Autoblindas of Armored Squadron Group 'Nizza'* from late 1941 in an experimental platoon. Note that the AS37 Autoblinda was equipped with Pirelli Type 'Raiflex' tires while the AB41 at its side has Pirelli Type 'Libya' tires. (Central State Archives)

▲ Front view of the *Carrozzeria Speciale on SPA-Viberti AS43* without armament inside the Officine Viberti factory in Turin. The vehicle features the classic three-tone 'Continental' camouflage and is equipped with Pirelli 'Artiglio' type tyres. (Officine Viberti)

▼ The same *Carrozzeria Speciale on SPA-Viberti AS43* without armament as in the previous picture. From this angle one can clearly see the supports for the hoe tools at the rear and the tank cap. (Officine Viberti)

▲ Interior of the *Carrozzeria Speciale on SPA-Viberti AS43*. The seats for the driver and commander are the same as those used on the AB series Autoblinde. The picture shows the internal skeleton onto which the armour plates were bolted. (Officine Viberti)

▼ Rear view of the crew compartment of the *Carrozzeria Speciale on SPA-Viberti AS43*. Attached to the rear flamethrower plate, the painted wooden racks for 8-round magazines for the main armament, below, fixed to the floor, the racks for 24-round magazines for the secondary armament. (Officine Viberti)

▲ Armoured vehicles of *Armoured Group M 'Leonessa'* deployed in Turin before the parade on 23 May 1944 through the streets of the city centre. Clearly visible are an L6/40 Tank, two *Carrozzeria Speciale on SPA-Viberti AS43*, an Autoblinda AB41 and an M Armoured Tank with their respective crews. At the bottom one can see a Lancia 3Ro while on the right one can see two OM Taurus. (Elvezio Borgatti)

▼ Two *Carrozzeria Speciali on SPA-Viberti AS43* followed by an Autoblinda AB41 in Piazza Carlo Felice, in front of Porta Nuova station in Turin during the parade on 23 May 1944. (Elvezio Borgatti)

▲ Also on 23 May 1944, the parade column passes between Piazza Carlo Felice and Via Roma. One can see an *Autoblinda AB41*, the two *Carrozzeria Speciale on SPA-Viberti AS43*, an L6/40 Tank and two M13/40 Tanks preceded by L3 Tanks of the M 'Leonessa' Armoured Group. (Elvezio Borgatti)

▼ The second M13/40 Tank of the column followed by the L6/40 Tank, the two *Carrozzeria Speciale on SPA-Viberti AS43*, the Autoblinda AB41 and another M Tank in Via Roma in Turin on 23 May 1944. (Elvezio Borgatti)

▲ The parade of the *Armoured Group M 'Leonessa'* enters Piazza Castello surrounded by two wings of the crowd. One can clearly see Palazzo Madama (right) and the Royal Palace (background). In the centre of the picture, the Monument to the Standard Bearer of the Sardinian Army covered by a wooden box filled with sand to prevent it being damaged by bombing. (Elvezio Borgatti)

▼ Detail of the *Carrozzeria Speciale on SPA-Viberti AS43* on parade on 23 May 1944. The vehicle has the number plate 'GNR 0151' and is in light Saharan khaki monochrome camouflage. On the hatch at the rear of the turret the department symbol is visible. On the sloping rear plate one can see the hoe tools and, further down, the trapdoor from which the spare wheel was inserted. (Elvezio Borgatti)

▲ A trumpeter of the *Gruppo Corazzato M 'Leonessa'* in front of a *Carrozzeria Speciale on SPA-Viberti AS43* parked together with a *SPA-Viberti Autoprotetta* armoured car in the courtyard of the 'Alessandro La Marmora' Barracks in Turin, home of the 1st 'Aristide Lissa' Tank Company of the *Gruppo Corazzato M 'Leonessa'*. One can clearly see the department badges and, in front of it on the wing, an obstruction pole to help the driver drive on narrow roads. The trumpeter is equipped with a Model 1939 Assailant's Dagger. (Nicola Pignato)

▲ A *Carrozzeria Speciale on SPA-Viberti AS43* parked in the courtyard of the 'Alessandro La Marmora' Barracks in Turin in front of an OM Taurus during maintenance. The soldier standing on the engine compartment holds with his left forearm the brush to clean the barrel of the Breda 20/65 Model 1935 cannon-mirror gun. Above the turret appears to be the Breda Model 1938 Medium Machine Gun, also under maintenance. The picture was taken shortly before the cannon was removed, as evidenced by the open rear hatch of the turret. (Elvezio Borgatti)

▼ Turin, Via Roma, 23 March 1945. The *Gruppo Corazzato M 'Leonessa'* (Armoured Group M) parades through the city for the last time on the occasion of the 28th anniversary of the founding of the Fasci di Combattimento (Fascist Combat Forces). A *Carrozzeria Speciale on a SPA-Viberti AS43*, here portrayed in front of a SPA-Viberti self-protected armoured car, takes part in the parade. The vehicle shows the three-tone camouflage adopted by the department from December 1944, it seems that the departmental badges were not covered by the new layers of paint.

▲ A *Carrozzeria Speciale on SPA-Viberti AS43* during a patrol of the Tirano area in late April 1945. The vehicle was part of the *Armoured Group M 'Leonessa'* detachment that moved from Turin to Valtellina to protect the access routes to the Republican Alpine Redoubt. (Giorgio Pisanò)

▼ A *Carrozzeria Speciale on SPA-Viberti AS43* in the hands of Tyrolean partisans, after the clashes in the mountain town. A patriotic inscription appears on the front of the vehicle, probably *'Liberation Army'*. (g.c. Ritter).

SPA-Viberti AS43 Autoprotected Armoured car

Less well known was the *SPA-Viberti AS43 Autoprotetta armoured car*[60], also an improvised vehicle on the chassis of the *SPA-Viberti AS43 armoured car*, used by the *Armoured Group M 'Leonessa'* in Piedmont[61].

Used as a troop transport vehicle, it retained the bodywork of the armoured car to which an armoured superstructure was added with an uncovered ceiling, which gave protection to the troops on board and allowed them to use their personal armament by exposing themselves outside the gauge. As with the *Carrozzeria Speciale on the SPA-Viberti AS43*, the assembly of the armoured structure was the work of Officine Viberti of Turin, as can be seen from a picture of the newly completed vehicle in the company's archives.

As with the special bodies, it is likely that the armour plates were delivered from the *Turin Army Arsenal* and installed by workers from some Turin factory[62].

For the *Autoprotette AS43*, the engine compartment was kept unchanged, without any modifications or armouring of any kind, decreasing its protection but, at the same time, decreasing the total weight of the vehicle.

The open armoured structure extended from the driver's cab to the rear of the vehicle and protected the occupants from small arms fire. This protection consisted of steel plates of very limited thickness, probably no more than 4.5 mm.

At the front, the front plate was divided into two sections, the right one, for the driver, had a small armoured window. This plate could be lowered at the front for greater visibility when driving through secure areas.

Instead, the left plate was fixed and a ball bearing for the armament was mounted in the centre. Behind the armoured windscreen were the access doors, and in fact a portion of the vehicle's side section was vertical, to make it easier to open the hatch, which was fitted with a slot.

The centre-rear section of the vehicle, where the transported soldiers sat, was slightly inclined to increase protection, and on each side there was a slit to check the battlefield without exposing themselves from the silhouette and to respond to enemy fire in the event of an ambush.

An almost unique feature of the vehicle was its fully welded structure, therefore without any bolts or internal metal skeleton.

The seven[63] men transported to the rear sat on side benches, while the rear gun was centrally positioned on another ball mount, identical to the front one. Thanks to the height of the armoured superstructure, the rear spare wheel was maintained without hindering the firing sector of the retreating gun.

---

[60] The vehicle is also called '*AS43 Protected*' in some publications.

[61] Given the improvised nature of the vehicle, there is no certain data on the total number of vehicles produced. However, iconographic sources confirm the presence of at least two examples.

[62] *Gli Autoveicoli da Combattimento dell'Esercito Italiano (1940-1945), Tomo I, Volume Two* reports how the vehicles were converted at the Officina Centrale or Autoparco della GNR in Piacenza. This hypothesis seems unlikely as the *'Leonessa'*, which was also deployed in Emilia Romagna, does not seem to have used the *SPA-Viberti AS43 Autoprotected Armoured cars* in that region.

[63] As with many details, sources are conflicting, *Gli Autoveicoli da Combattimento dell'Esercito Italiano (1940-1945), Tomo I, Volume Two* on page 454 gives the number of men carried as 6 + 2 crew members while at least one photo from the period shows a total of 9 men on board the vehicle, including the 2 crew members.

Apart from the small core transported, the crew consisted of the driver on the right and the captain on the left.

The on-board armament consisted of two *Breda Model 1937 medium machine guns* operated frontally by the vehicle commander and at the rear by one of the soldiers carried on board. A total of 2,000 8 mm cartridges in 100 20-round plates were carried in a rack positioned between the commander and the driver and in two small racks above the side lockers[64]. We can assume that the side lockers contained additional machine gun magazines given the absence of heavy armament. Both machine guns were detachable from the ball mounts and could be used on the ground by means of two tripods carried on two mounts fixed above the front mudguards after removing the front gasoline canister racks.

The first public appearance of the *self-protected SPA-Viberti AS43s took* place on 23 July 1944[65] for a parade of *Armoured Group M 'Leonessa'* in Milan. On that occasion, a formation company of the *'Leonessa'* was sent to Milan with several wheeled vehicles (including a *Carrozzeria Speciale on SPA-Viberti AS43*) and armoured vehicles, which, after receiving the war flag from Gen. Ricci, paraded through the city.

Even for the *SPA-Viberti AS43 Autoprotetta armoured car,* the history of its service in anti-partisan actions is not precisely known, but we can, with certainty, trace the final fate of the two vehicles whose existence we have evidence of.

A first specimen was lost during an *anti-Partisan* operation organised by the commander of the *Anti-Partisan Regiment*, Colonel Alessandro Ruta, which began on 6 March 1945.

Leading the action was Major Gino Cera, commander of the Turin GNR *Public Order Battalion,* and included a column of units from Turin a platoon of the *1st Tank Company*, with an *AB41 Armoured Carriage* and a *SPA-Viberti AS43 Self-protected Armoured car,* two platoons of the *3rd Arditi Company*, some units of the *Anti-Partisan Regiment* with a *Lancia Lince* reconnaissance armoured car[66], about 80 squads from the *1st Black Brigade 'Ather Capelli'*, a company from the Turin *Public Order Battalion*, the *1ª Company* of the GNR's *XXIXth Assault 'M' Battalion*, the *Arditi Sciatori Company*, the RAP's *Genio Platoon*, and 25 marines from the *'Umberto Cumero' Detachment*[67] of the *10th MAS Division*.

From Alba came the *5ª Company* of the *2nd RAP Battalion*, a platoon of the *8ª Company* and two *75/13 Model 1915 cannons* from a battery of the *10th Group*, as well as a platoon of the *Arditi Ufficiali Division* from Bra, for a total of about 350 soldiers and auxiliary personnel[68]. Partisan forces in the area were estimated at around 1,000 partisans[69].

---

64 The side racks were outside the armoured structure and therefore not accessible to the crew in the event of an enemy attack.

65 The parade was organised by General Renato Ricci, Commander of the *Republican National Guard,* to 'mock' the coup d'état of the year before that had deposed Mussolini.

66 The vehicle does not appear in official sources but there is a photo of it after its capture by partisans in Cisterna d'Asti. S. Corbatti and M. Nava, ...*Come il Diamante! I Carristi Italiani 1943-'45*, Bruxelles Laran Edition, 2008, p. 73, op. cit. in bibliography.

67 Formed by elements of the 10th MAS Division in March 1944 with the strength of one company; it was under the command of Lieutenant Aldo Campani. The detachment's task was to defend the FIAT plants. The detachment was requested by FIAT engineer Valletta. Replaced in October 1944 by the RAP, it merged into the 'Torino' Detachment of the 10th MAS Division.

68 The complete staff of the column is mentioned by P. Crippa, *Storia dei Reparti Corazzati della Repubblica Sociale Italiana*, Milan, Marcia Edizioni, October 2022, p. 87-88, op. cit. in bibliography and by L. Sandri, *Raggruppamento Anti Partigiani (RAP), Reparto Arditi Ufficiali (RAU), Una Documentazione,* Milan, self-published, 2020, op. cit. in bibliography.

69 The partisan units were: *6th Autonomous Alpine Division 'Asti'* with three brigades, *Matteotti Division 'Three*

The action was aimed at combing the province of Asti on the border with the province of Cuneo[70]. After an initial clash in Valmellana on 6 March that cost the lives of 17 squadrists[71] of the *1st Black Brigade 'Ather Capelli'* and several wounded, the operation continued with heavy clashes in Cisterna d'Asti that did not end until 7 March 1945.

After passing through Santo Stefano Roero, between the afternoon of 8 and the morning of 9 March, the column of republican troops was ambushed by partisan forces just outside the village.

The *AB41 Autoblinda* commanded by Second Lieutenant Fossati was the opening vehicle in the column, behind the armoured car was a *FIAT 666NM armoured car* with a two-axle trailer full of soldiers, followed by the *SPA-Viberti AS43 Autoprotetta armoured car* of Second Lieutenant Bruno Berneschi, and then other Armoured cars and cars full of soldiers and the *Lancia Lince Auotoblinda* of the RAP.

The column was ambushed as it left the village and almost immediately, bullets perforated one of the tyres of the armoured car under the command of Lieutenant Fossati, immobilising it.

The *FIAT 666NM armoured car* was also fired upon, killing some soldiers and starting a fire. Lieutenant Berneschi, ordered the driver of the self-protected armoured car to overtake the blocked AB41 to support the ambushed fascist soldiers and keep the partisans occupied with suppressive fire. The *SPA-Viberti AS43 self-protected armoured car* began to move and open fire, Sub-Lieutenant Berneschi was wounded in the eye while handling the front gun, while the vehicle, hit by several bursts of small arms fire. Berneschi then ordered the transported soldiers out of the protected vehicle and continued to open fire with the machine gun to cover them.

When he tried to retreat, in pulling his weapon from the ball mount, he exposed himself outside the outline of the vehicle and was hit by an automatic weapon discharge. Immediately rescued by soldiers, he was brought to cover but expired after being ordered to retreat[72].

The remaining vehicles and troops reached the nearby town of Canale, abandoning several vehicles, including the FIAT 666NM now engulfed in flames with its trailer, the *SPA-Viberti AS43 Autoprotetta armoured car* also in flames, the *Lancia Lince* of the RAP and at least one civilian vehicle, a FIAT 508C damaged by partisan fire.

Second Lieutenant Fossati, wounded while trying to replace a punctured tyre, was rescued by his crew and managed to retreat with the armoured car, which did not fall into partisan hands.

Apart from Second Lieutenant Berneschi, the fascists suffered three casualties and many wounded. On 9 March, with the help of some artillery pieces of the *Anti-Partisan Regiment* from Turin, the fascist forces regained control of the area[73].

Boundaries' with five brigades and *103rd Garibaldi Brigade 'Rolandino'*.
70 The raking included the municipalities of San Damiano d'Asti, Montà, Santo Stefano Roero, Cisterna d'Asti and Baldissera d'Alba.
71 According to L. Sandri, *Raggruppamento Anti Partigiani (RAP), Reparto Arditi Ufficiali (RAU), Una Documentazione*, Milan, self-published, 2020, op. cit. in bibliography, there were 18 dead in addition to 6 captured and later shot by partisans and 11 wounded.
72 For more on the Battle of Santo Stefano Roero and the death of Second Lieutenant Berneschi see the book *...Come il Diamante! I Carristi Italiani 1943-'45*, Bruxelles Laran Edition, 2008, p. 175, op. cit. in bibliography.
73 In total, fascist losses in the four-day operation were 27 dead and 32 wounded. Partisan casualties are a matter of debate, sources of the time speak of 108 dead while to date there are only 3 dead and an unknown

The second *Camionetta SPA-Viberti AS43 Autoprotetta* instead took part in the parade of 23 March 1945[74] in Turin, parading through the streets of the Piedmont capital for the last time. In the photos taken on this occasion, the new three-tone camouflage can be seen, with dark green and reddish-brown patches on the original light Saharan khaki that did not cover the departmental symbol on the mudguards and side plates.

On 25 April 1945, the great partisan insurrection began, but was delayed by one day in Turin[75]. On 26 April, the regional *National Liberation Committee* issued the order *'Aldo Dice 26x1'* and the *Patriotic Action Squads* and *Patriotic Action Groups* units, supported by a few partisan nuclei that entered the city, occupied the infrastructure in the suburbs and managed to push their way into the city centre.

The headquarters of the *'Gazzetta del Popolo', the* Prefecture and even the Town Hall were occupied, while furious gunfights began at the EIAR headquarters and the Casa Littoria.

By the evening, and throughout 27 April, there were heavy clashes with the fascist forces who counter-attacked, reoccupying the headquarters of the *'Gazzetta del Popolo'*, the Town Hall and the Prefecture, while the EIAR headquarters was never occupied by the partisans. On the evening of 27 April 1945, the request to surrender presented to the *Italian Social Republic* troops by Monsignor Garneri[76] was refused, but it was decided to prepare an organised retreat towards Lombardy, to head for the *Republican Alpine Redoubt* in Valtellina following the *'Z2-B - Sudden'* plan.

The choice was not dictated by a lack of men or food and ammunition, but also by the lack of communication with other fascist divisions in other Italian cities. The Turin officers were unaware that most of the remaining cities in northern Italy had already capitulated or were in much more desperate situations than that of the Piedmontese capital.

Piazza Castello, Turin's main square, was chosen as the rallying point, where the fascist units with most of their personnel, some family members and a few German units converged.

All the vehicles of the still functioning Italian divisions, both armoured vehicles and Armoured cars, were also brought to the square, loaded to the hilt with ammunition, provisions and fuel.

A column was organised under the command of Colonel Giovanni Cabras[77] with the approximately 5,000[78] people present. At the head and rear of the column were the armoured vehicles of the *1st Tank Company* of the *'Leonessa'* and at the rear the *1st Arditi Ufficiali Department* of the RAP.

---

number of wounded.

74 The parade was organised in honour of the 28th anniversary of the founding of the Fasci di Combattimento.

75 The insurrection in Turin was delayed by a day with respect to the general partisan uprising because Colonel John Melior Stevens, commander of the Allied Mission in Piedmont feared a bloodbath after the words of German General Ernst Schlemmer, commander of the Axis forces with still 75,000 men under his command between Piedmont and Liguria, who threatened to *'Transform Turin into a second Warsaw'*. Col. Stevens tried to cancel the attack on Turin, delaying it for a day but finally having to give in to partisan audacity.

76 Monsignor Giuseppe Garneri, rector of Turin Cathedral, was sent by the Cardinal of Turin, Maurilio Fossati and the CLN to negotiate the surrender.

77 Giovanni Cabras, provincial commander of the Piedmontese UPI and commander of the Turin Provincial Military Command. He commanded the column that reached the free zone of Strambino from Turin.

78 These were only Italians from various fascist units, politicians and officials, as well as civilians and family members of soldiers. Most of the Germans present in the city took other routes, joining the retreating German divisions from Val Susa or Liguria that did not enter Turin to avoid being stranded in the city.

No precise data are available, but the *SPA-Viberti AS43 self-protected armoured car was part of the* column took part in the retreat, which began at 1:40 a.m. on 28 April 1945, in light rain.

Reaching the Dora river, the vanguards of the *Armoured Group M 'Leonessa'* broke through a partisan barricade in Corso Giulio Cesare supported by a *75/13 Model 1915 Cannon* of the *10th Artillery Group*, in the clash 2 men of the *1st Armed Officers' Department* were killed. Continuing on towards Milan on the A4 motorway, the column reached Chivasso at dawn. From Chivasso, the column began to take side roads because it was too exposed to Allied air attacks; in changing roads, the small group of Germans broke away from the column and continued on their own towards Milan.

On the morning of 29th April 1945, the column reached Cigliano where it was subjected to machine-gun fire from Allied aircraft. Apparently, there were no fatalities or vehicles destroyed although, on the way, a armoured car skidded and overturned resulting in the death of some occupants.

After a day's march on the evening of 29 April, the column stayed overnight in Livorno Ferraris where the units learned of Mussolini's death.

Having reached Valtellina, they opted to reach Strambino Romano, a free zone where they waited for the Allies to hand themselves over to them.

Once Strambino was reached, after a few days of waiting, in which other departments, fascists and Germans joined the troops in Turin to wait for the allied divisions, on 5 May 1945, General Adami Rossi[79], head of the troops in the free zone, signed the surrender of the Italian troops with the allied troops. Between 15 and 20,000 men had amassed in Strambino Romano[80] and among the thousands of vehicles handed over to the allies was the last example of the *SPA-Viberti AS43 Autoprotetta armoured car*, whose final fate is unfortunately unknown.

---

[79] General Enrico Adami Rossi, commander of the Piedmont Regional Military Command, signed the surrender of the Italian troops in the free zone of Strambino Romano.

[80] The number, reported by most sources, was actually higher: in addition to the 5,000 republicans who arrived from Turin, the *5th Gebirgsjäger-Division* arrived in the Strambino Romano area with 16,775 German soldiers and 3,517 Italians and Russians with 124 various artillery pieces, 615 machine guns, 12 Panzer IVs, 12 self-propelled and 9 Italian-made armoured cars, 1,255 motor vehicles and 5,511 animals.

The *34. Infanterie-Division* with its 10,000 personnel stood 15 km further north together with the Imperia *OP Company* and the *'Cacciatori degli Appennini' Regiment*. Data taken from L. Sandri, *La 5^ Gebirgs Division sul Fronte Italiano 1943-1945: Una Documentazione*, op. cit. in bibliography and M. Nava, *La 34^ Infanterie Division sul Fronte Italiano: 1943-1945*, op. cit. in bibliography.

▲ An example of the *SPA-Viberti AS43 Autoprotetta armoured car* under maintenance. In this picture, one can see the badge on the wing, the two tripods of the Breda Model 1937 Medium Machine Guns, the Pirelli 'Artiglio' type tyres, the starter crank attached to the bracket on the armoured car guard, the front plate for the driver with bulletproof glass and the door on the left side of the vehicle. All soldiers are equipped with M33 helmets and wear the short grey-green two-pocket jacket, introduced in Spring 1944, under which they wear a black shirt. The trousers are similar to those of the tank men but with large pockets at the knees, which are inserted directly into the boot like the paratrooper model. (Elvezio Borgatti)

▲ Another picture of the *SPA-Viberti AS43 self-protected armoured car* with 9 soldiers on board in Spring 1944. From this angle, the armoured locker above the tank, left unprotected, and the slit on the side of the vehicle are clearly visible. The militiamen of the Armoured Group M 'Leonessa' who probably went out on patrol, are equipped with M33 helmets, including the driver who also has motorbike goggles. (Nino Arena)

▼ Rear view of a *SPA-Viberti AS43 self-protected armoured car*. The ball mount for the Breda Model 1937 Medium Machine Gun is clearly visible at the rear of the armoured superstructure. The rear wooden compartment and spare wheel remain unchanged, as do the armoured locker and tank. (Officine Viberti)

▲ A *SPA-Viberti AS43 self-protected armoured car* of the Gruppo Corazzato M 'Leonessa' formation company sent to Milan for the parade on 23 July 1944, the anniversary of the Grand Council that declared Fascism to have fallen. The Arditi on board wear the new dark blue German cut uniform and beret. The vehicle is photographed in Piazza Duomo, and probably closed the column of armoured vehicles, in fact a FIAT 626NM armoured car and a FIAT 666NM are clearly visible behind the armoured car. (Elvezio Borgatti)

▼ A picture taken after the battle of Santo Stefano Roero on 8 March 1945. The vehicle in question is undoubtedly Lieutenant Berneschi's *SPA-Viberti AS43 self-protected armoured car*, which was probably overturned to clear the road after the clash. The tyres are missing, devoured by the flames of the fire that developed on the vehicle.

▲ A *SPA-Viberti AS43 self-protected armoured car* with the number plate 'GNR 438' of the *Gruppo Corazzato M 'Leonessa'* during the parade of 23 March 1945 in Via Roma in Turin followed by a FIAT 666NM armoured car of the same department.

▼ *SPA-Viberti AS43 self-protected armoured car* of *Armoured Group M 'Leonessa'* during the same parade. The vehicle received three-tone camouflage that did not cover the departmental badges on the wing. The soldiers wore black berets and a black uniform modelled on the German tank uniform introduced in 1942.

▲ Some vehicles of the Axis troops that surrendered at Strambino Romano on 5 May 1945 guarding an American soldier of the 34th Infantry Division. One can clearly see an M42 Self-Propelled Command Tank, four M15/42 Tanks and one M14/41 Tank. Behind the rows of armoured vehicles, the silhouette of a *SPA-Viberti AS43 self-protected armoured car* can be seen on the left. In addition to the armoured vehicles, two FIAT 626NLM Armoured cars, a FIAT-SPA 38R, a Lancia 3Ro and two Autoblinde AB43 can be distinguished. (Elvezio Borgatti)

▼ The FIAT 666NM armoured car after the fighting in Santo Stefano Roero. As the *SPA-Viberti AS43 self-protected armoured car*, the vehicle was heavily damaged by the flames. (Courtesy of Paolo Crippa)

▲ The heavy unified trailer pulled by the FIAT 666NM armoured car during the Santo Stefano Roero clashes, also on the side of the road, completely destroyed. (Courtesy of Paolo Crippa)

▼ A late-series FIAT 508C is wrecked and overturned on the side of the road after the March 1945 fighting in Santo Stefano Roero. It too, like all the other vehicles, bears the marks of fire. (Courtesy of Paolo Crippa)

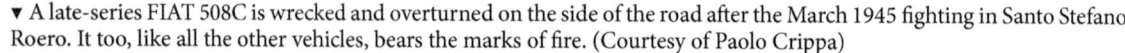

SPA-Viberti AS43 Armoured Armoured car

Not only did the *Republican National Guard* use the *SPA-Viberti AS43 armoured car* chassis as the basis of its improvised vehicles, but also the *X^a MAS Division* of the *Republican National Navy*.

The *1^a Company* of the *'Lightning' Battalion*, created in March 1944 and commanded by Lieutenant Colonel Luigi Carallo had at least one handcrafted armoured armoured car in service in his unit, the so-called *SPA-Viberti AS43 Armoured Armoured car*.

The *'Lightning' Battalion*, the majority of which was made up of soldiers who had belonged to the Bersaglieri speciality before the armistice, consisted of three companies and was equipped with three FIAT 1100 vans and a homemade armoured FIAT 1100, at least one OM Taurus light armoured car, a Bianchi Miles, three 81 mm mortars and two Swiss Solothurn S-18/1000 anti-tank guns[81].

According to the above-mentioned report of the *Turin Army Arsenal of* 23 March 1945, the *X^a MAS Division* received, among other things, *'two shields and self-protected armament'*. One of the two shields certainly went to equip the *AS43 Blindata*, while the second had an unknown fate.

According to the testimony of Maurizio Gamberini[82], a veteran of the *'Fulmine' Battalion*, the armoured body was assembled by FIAT workers after their shifts at one of the company's plants in Turin, unfortunately not specifying which one in his account.

Many sources report that the chassis could have been that of a *SPA-Viberti AS42 Camionetta*, but from the pictures we can deduce that the vehicle was on a *SPA-Viberti AS43* chassis due to the presence of the front engine compartment and the smaller dimensions compared to the *Camionetta AS42*.

An armoured superstructure was attached to the frame, partly welded, partly bolted.

Starting at the front, the engine compartment had an angled armature with a radiator grille and some upper inspection hatches.

At the front of the cockpit was the driver on the right and the commander on the left, with a ball-mounted machine gun at his disposal.

The fighting compartment that comprised the entire middle and rear of the vehicle had a superstructure behind the driver's and commander's positions where two more machine guns were placed, one in front and one in retreat[83].

To access and exit the vehicle there was probably a rear door, of which unfortunately there are no photographic sources.

Above the commander's position, on the left, was a trapdoor used to control the battlefield, while a second trapdoor was on the top of the superstructure and was used to operate the searchlight at the front.

The wheel guards were removed and replaced with armoured models, longer than the originals and of a different shape, with the headlights recessed inside. These also covered the tyres to protect them from small arms fire. The wing side plates could be opened to change

---

81 Equipment visible during the public appearance on 29 October 1944 in Turin and in other photos.
82 Testimony reported in *...Like the Diamond*, p. 100, op. cit. in bibliography.
83 No photographs of the rear of the vehicle have survived and the presence of the machine gun in the retreat is still only speculated upon. The weapon does, however, appear in several illustrations presented by various publications in recent years.

tyres or for suspension maintenance.

The armour of the armoured car was very light, which could mean that the thickness was very limited, between 4 mm and 6 mm.

This meant that, despite its bulk, the vehicle had limited weight while maintaining a certain speed on the road as far as possible.

The camouflage of the *SPA-Viberti AS43 Armoured Armoured car was in* three tones already seen on the vehicles mentioned above, light Saharan khaki with dark green and reddish brown spots.

The first time the vehicle was photographed was on 29 October 1944, during a parade in Turin, on the occasion of the handing over of the war flag of the *'Fulmine' Battalion*. The *SPA-Viberti AS43 Armoured Armoured car* paraded, together with the other vehicles of the battalion, along Via Roma and then reached Piazza Castello, where the unit was inspected in the courtyard of the Royal Palace by a number of officers who handed over the war flag. A few days earlier, on 10 October 1944, partisan units[84] of the *1st Alpine Divisions Group* under the command of Enrico 'Mauri' Martini entered the town of Alba[85], 50 km south of Turin, creating the *Partisan Republic of Alba*, which remained free and autonomous for 23 days.

On 30 October, Colonel Alessandro Ruta of the RAP received orders from the Extraordinary Commissioner for Piedmont, Paolo Zerbino to reoccupy Alba. In addition to the 600 RAP men deployed in Turin and Bra, Col. Ruta asked for and obtained reinforcements from the Black Brigades, the GNR and the X^a *MAS Division*.

On 2 November 1944, under the command of Colonel Alessandro Ruta, the *Italian Social Republic units* including: training units of the *1st Black Brigade 'Ather Capelli'* of Turin and the *5th Black Brigade 'Carlo Lidonnici'* of Cuneo, the *1st Officers' Armed Forces Unit* and a platoon of the *2nd Officers' Armed Forces Unit of* the RAP, the *10th Special Battalion* the *'Lupo' Battalion* and the *'Fulmine' Battalion*, the *'Da Giussano'* and *'San Giorgio' Field Artillery Groups* of the *10th MAS Division* and some divisions of the *M Armoured Group 'Leonessa'*[86] for a total of about 1,000 soldiers attacked the partisan republic to reoccupy Alba.

The forces were divided into three columns: the north column crossed the Tanaro by swimming, on boats and from the Mussotto footbridge, aiming at Alba via Porta Tanaro and Porta Cherasco. The east column, with the support of armoured units was to conquer some farmsteads south-east of Alba and then move towards Porta Savona and support the advance of the north column on Porta Cherasco with an armoured detachment. The last column, the south-west, was to proceed to occupy some farmsteads and then advance on the Alba-Roddi roadway to block any attempt to retreat south-west[87].

---

84 Around 2,000 partisans, mainly belonging to the *2nd Autonomous Division 'Langhe'*, took part in the attack.
85 In Alba, from 3 October, there was a garrison of 300 Alpine soldiers under the command of Lieutenant Colonel Ippolito Radaelli of the *'Cadore' Alpine Battalion*. The 300 men withdrew after an agreement with the partisans, taking all their weapons and equipment with them.
86 The *'Leonessa'* detached three tanks and two armoured vehicles for the taking of Alba, as mentioned in ...*Come il Diamante*, p. 171. In addition to the *AS43 Armoured Armoured car*, the X^a *MAS Division* also employed an L6/40 Tank from the *'Lupo' Battalion* but without the 20 mm cannon.
87 F. Barbano, *I Fatti Militari di Alba in alcuni Documenti Partigiani e Repubblicani (10 October 1944-15 April 1945)*, MLI, Number 4, January 1950, p. 29, op. cit. in bibliography.

The partisan units defending the city were the *2nd Autonomous Division 'Langhe'*, the *1st Partisan Brigade 'Castellino'* and the *23ª Partisan Brigade 'Canale'* of the *1st Alpine Divisions Group*, the *48th Garibaldi Brigade 'Dante Di Nanni'* and the *78th Garibaldi Brigade 'Devic'*.

After several hours of fighting, the city was reoccupied by fascist troops around noon. The *SPA-Viberti AS43 Armoured Armoured car* was transported to Alba, although it was probably not used in the attack on the partisan lines due to the impossibility of ferrying armoured vehicles across the Tanaro river. It therefore remained on the north bank of the Tanaro, providing, if possible, fire support to the Fascist troops attacking[88]. After a strenuous defence, Alba was recaptured by the fascist forces and the first vehicles entered the town[89].

After the actions in Alba, the *'Fulmine' Battalion* operated in the Asti area and on 12 November 1944, it was deployed in an anti-partisan action in Locana, in Val d'Orco 90 km from Asti, which had been occupied by partisans.

The vehicle was commanded by Officer Cadet Sergeant Filippo Prestipino, and the conductor was Maroon Rino Pazzi. The crew was completed by Officer Cadet Sergeant Gianni Schietti and Marine Maurizio Cannella[90].

At the end of the year, the *'Lightning' Battalion* was transferred to Veneto, to the area of Conegliano Veneto where it fought against the Slovenian partisans of Tito's *IXth Corps*. According to veteran testimonies, the *SPA-Viberti AS43 Armoured Armoured car was* also transferred to Veneto, arriving 2 days after the unit, but due to the Karst terrain and the lack of spare parts, the vehicle was abandoned in the barracks and never used again.

---

88 Although it is certainly not a granitic source as it is fictional, it is worth mentioning the presence of *'two large half-armoured cars'* used by the republican troops when entering Alba after the partisan retreat, cited by Beppe Fenoglio in *Il Partigiano Johnny,* Turin, Einaudi, 2014, p. 303.
89 As far as losses are concerned, there are conflicting sources: the official report of the RSI spoke of 4 Republican deaths and 10 wounded, against 29 partisans killed, 30 'probable', 10 passed by the arms, 14 captured and 40 suspects apprehended in addition to around 80 wounded. On the other hand, Monsignor Luigi Maria Grassi, Bishop of Alba reported 4 fascist dead and 4 partisans plus another 4 wounded partisans. F. Barbano, *I Fatti Militari di Alba in alcuni Documenti Partigiani e Repubblicani (10 October 1944-15 April 1945)*, MLI, Number 4, January 1950, p. 34, op. cit. in bibliography.
90 P. Crippa, *Storia dei Reparti Corazzati della Repubblica Sociale Italiana,* Milan, Marcia Edizioni, October 2022, p. 139, op. cit. in bibliography.

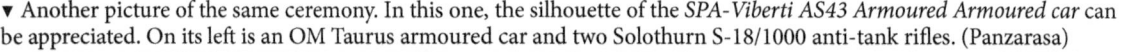

▲ Marò of the *X MAS Division* parade during the ceremony in which the department pennants were received on 29 October 1944 in Turin's Piazzetta Reale. From the right of the picture, some vehicles belonging to the 1st Company of the 'Fulmine' Battalion can be seen: the engine compartment of the *SPA-Viberti AS43 Armoured Armoured car*, three FIAT 1100s, a FIAT 508CM and some motorbikes. In front of the vehicles, three Model 1935 81mm mortars. (Panzarasa)

▼ Another picture of the same ceremony. In this one, the silhouette of the *SPA-Viberti AS43 Armoured Armoured car* can be appreciated. On its left is an OM Taurus armoured car and two Solothurn S-18/1000 anti-tank rifles. (Panzarasa)

▲ ▼ Two pictures of Marò from the 1st Company of the 'Fulmine' Battalion posing in front of the *SPA-Viberti AS43 Armoured Armoured car* at Locana on 12 November 1944. Unfortunately in the pictures the vehicle is only partially visible, nevertheless, in the second picture behind the barrel of the MAB38 of the soldier on the left, one can glimpse part of what appears to be the rear hatch of the armoured car. (Panzarasa)

▲ The *SPA-Viberti AS43 Armoured Armoured car* in Via Roma in Turin parades after the unit received its pennants on 29 October 1944. From the picture, the crewmen can clearly be seen through the open doors. (Panzarasa)

▼ A armoured car column of the 1ˢᵗ Company of the 'Fulmine' Battalion advances towards the village of Locana in Piedmont on 12 November 1944. Unfortunately, the angle of the shot does not allow us to identify the Armoured cars of the unit. Instead, the *SPA-Viberti AS43 Armoured Armoured car* and the *FIAT 1100 Protetta*, nicknamed 'V2' by the Marò because of the noise it emitted when the engine was running, are recognisable. (Panzarasa)

▲ The same image enlarged to appreciate the clumsy silhouette of the *SPA-Viberti AS43 Armoured Armoured car* of the 1st Company of the 'Lightning' Battalion. (Panzarasa)

SPA-Viberti AS43 Armoured Ambulance

The need for a protected ambulance in service to evacuate the wounded on the battlefields was already seen in the very early years of the war during operations in North Africa together with the need for armoured troop transport vehicles. Only after the armistice of 8 September 1943, however, was a shielded ambulance designed for Italian troops.

The design was developed by Officine Viberti[91] in Turin after the development of the *Carrozzeria Speciale on SPA-Viberti AS43* in 1944.

In view of the situation of the Italian troops at the end of the conflict, Viberti's engineers simplified the development by using part of the special armoured body structure and the *FIAT-SPA S37 Autoprotetto* developed in April 1941.

It is not clear why the Officine Viberti design office took the decision to use the armoured superstructure of the *S37 Autoprotetto*. The S37s were assembled at the SPA factory in Turin where there were probably still some armoured superstructures[92] and starting from these

---

91 N. Pignato, F. Cappellano, *Gli Autoveicoli da Combattimento dell'Esercito Italiano (1940-1945), Tomo I, Volume Secondo*, Roma, USSME, 2002, p. 454, op. cit. in bibliography.

92 On 24 May 1941, 200 *FIAT-SPA S37 Autoprotetti* were ordered, of which only 150 were delivered, so it is plausible that a small batch of superstructures was still at the SPA.

▲ The *FIAT-SPA S37 self-protected armoured car* taken during testing at the Rome DMV Study and Experience Center. The *SPA-Viberti AS43 Armoured Ambulance* would retain the same engine compartment and similar rear superstructure, but would be mounted on the chassis of a *SPA-Viberti AS43 armoured car* instead of the *FIAT-SPA AS37*.(USSME)

loose parts, an eventual prototype could have been assembled, saving on raw materials, time and assembly cost.

Unfortunately, the design remained only on paper and we cannot say much about its features. Although the superstructure was inherited from the Autos, the engine, suspension and mudguards remained unchanged from the *SPA-Viberti AS43 Armoured carettes*. The armoured structure was longer than that of the *Special Body on SPA-Viberti AS43* and less angular than that of the *S37 Autoprotetti in* order to increase the internal volume of the vehicle.

At the front, behind the engine compartment, was the driver on the right and the commander, probably a medical officer, on the left.

The commander had no access door as a spare wheel carrier was mounted on the left side. The armoured door, in two sections, was exclusively on the right side while at the rear there was a large central door, also divided into two sections, for easy boarding and disembarkation of stretcher bearers.

We are certain of the presence of a seat next to the driver as, on the original plans of the vehicle, two slots can be seen, one for the driver and one for a second man, absent on the *FIAT-SPA S37 Autoprotetto* and the *Autoblinda AS37*.

From the original drawings it appears that the vehicle was equipped with two stretcher supports on the left and three seats on the right for less seriously wounded and stretcher bearers[93]. The two stretcher supports, placed one on top of the other, could be reclined against

---

93 Unfortunately, there are no precise data on the crew of the vehicle, it is possible that the driver also acted as

the armoured structure to reduce bulk when not in use[94].

The sloping roof of the armoured superstructure could be opened, probably to let light into the sanitary compartment, which lacked internal electric lights.

As far as protection is concerned, nothing is known to us about the thickness of the vehicle's armour, but sharing parts of the armoured superstructure with the *FIAT-SPA S37 Autoprotetto*, we can assume that the armour was of similar thickness, i.e. between 8.5 mm and 6 mm, adequate to protect the crew and wounded from small arms fire and artillery shrapnel. As far as the total weight is concerned, we can assume that it would not deviate much from that of the 5.3-ton *FIAT-SPA S37 Autoprotetto*, while the speed and range could be comparable to that of the *Special Body on SPA-Viberti AS43*, sharing its engine and traction components. Obviously, the reduced weight of around one tonne would have increased the ambulance's performance, even if only slightly.

Unfortunately, due to the desperate conditions in the Italian Social Republic, the development of the shielded ambulance stopped at a paper project and was not even proposed to Italian or German officials. Certainly an interesting and unique self-protected vehicle, as the only similar vehicles were the German Sd.Kfz. 251 Krankenpanzerwagen (Armoured Ambulance) which, however, were nothing more than simple troop transport half-tracks with minor internal modifications. Had it been designed and presented before the Armistice of 8 September 1943, it could have facilitated the evacuation of wounded soldiers on the battlefield, saving the lives of many soldiers.

The *Gruppo Arditi Camionettisti Italiani*

Like the soldiers of the *1ª Legionary Armoured Division 'M'*, other Italian soldiers did not accept the armistice of 8 September 1943 with the Allied forces.

Among the units that from the very beginning decided to continue fighting the Germans were some companies of the *10th Arditi Regiment*[95].

The *112th Compagnia Camionettisti d'Assalto*[96] of the *2nd Battalion* and the *133rd Compagnia Camionettisti d'Assalto*[97] of the *3rd Battalion*[98] of the *10th Arditi Regiment*. The two companies moved from Santa Severa (the unit's headquarters) towards Rome with an unclear number of *SPA-Viberti AS42 'Metropolitane' Armoured cars*[99]. On the way to Rome, various groups

---

a stretcher-bearer to reduce the number of crew members to 3 (driver/bearer, doctor and second stretcher-bearer) in order to be able to transport up to 4 wounded (two on stretchers, two seated).

94 If necessary, the crew could have spread a single stretcher on the lower support and used it as a makeshift bench to seat more of the less seriously injured.

95 The *10th Arditi Regiment was created* on 26 April 1942, initially with battalion strength and called the *1st Special Arditi Battalion*, and with the subsequent creation of three more battalions. Each battalion had three companies, one consisting of paratroopers, one of swimmers and a third of armoured car drivers. L. E. Longo, *I "Reparti Speciali" Nella Seconda Guerra Mondiale*, Milan, Mursia, 1991, p. 108-109, op. cit. in bibliography.

96 Each *Armoured car Company* was on 4 patrols. Each patrol consisted of 2 officers and 18 arditi and was equipped with 6 armoured carettes. E. Finazzer and L. Carretta, *Le Camionette del Regio Esercito*, Trento, Gruppo Modellistico Trentino, 2014, p. 33-34. op. cit. in bibliography.

97 After Mussolini's arrest on 25 July 1943, the *'Young Fascists' Regiment*, made up of young men who had escaped capture in North Africa after being repatriated because they were wounded or suffering from malaria, was disbanded. Many young men asked and obtained to be included in the *10th Arditi Regiment*. The *133ª Assault Armoured car Company* was then created while others were probably assigned to other companies.

98 Many sources give conflicting data, we will just name the two companies that are cited by all sources.

99 Sources report a minimum of 6 to a maximum of 9 Armoured cars with which the volunteers presented themselves to the German troops in Rome.

of Italian units loyal to the German ally joined the volunteer squad. Arriving in the capital on 18 September 1943 with a total force of around 300 volunteers[100], Paris contacted the *2. Fallschirmjäger-Division 'Ramcke'*[101] and succeeded in having his men from the German division integrated.

The volunteers were immediately deployed for public order in the Italian capital, also garrisoning the EIAR headquarters and settling, with the rest of the German division, in Castel di Decima outside Rome[102].

At that point, a total of 107 Italian volunteers were framed in the German paratrooper division, of which 47 Arditi were placed under the command of Captain Paolo Paris assisted by Lieutenant Pania[103] and equipped with Armoured cars. Of the remaining approximately 200 volunteers, nothing is known. They were probably reassigned to other units of the newly formed *Italian Social Republic*.

The unit under the command of Capt. Paris was renamed *Gruppo Arditi Camionettisti Italiani* or *Spähungs-Abteilung 'Paris'*[104]. The group, which was used as a reconnaissance unit, was divided into two sections, each with a German officer acting as interpreter, and retained the Italian uniforms at first.

In October 1943, the unit took part in a training session of the *2nd Fallschirmjäger-Division* near the Colli Albani, south-east of Rome, before being transferred to the Eastern Front, following the German unit at the end of the month.

The transfer by rail was slowed down by Allied bombardment and bad weather conditions, and it was not until mid-November that the *Arditi Camionettisti* arrived in the Ukrainian town of Žytomyr[105], in time to take part in defensive actions against the Red Army, supporting the first fighting 40 km from Kiev.

Due to the scarcity of material, the Camionettisti supplemented their clothing with Luftwaffe and Heer uniforms to which, however, the Arditi frieze and the Young Fascists' badge were pinned, by concession of the German division headquarters.

Between 3 and 13 November 1943, the Second Battle of Kiev was fought and the Soviets launched a small series of offensives shortly afterwards as a prelude to a larger offensive.

In mid-December, the *Gruppo Arditi Camionettisti Italiani* followed two companies of the *2. Fallschirmjäger-Division* in an aerial transfer to Kirovohrad[106] acting as reinforcements to repel the Soviet advance. Joined by the rest of the paratroop division and the armoured carettes, the Italian soldiers and their vehicles were assigned to four companies of the *2. Fallschirmjäger-Division at* the end of the month, thus ceasing to exist as an organic unit[107].

---

100 Of the approximately 300 volunteers, more than a hundred came from the *10th Regiment Arditi, the* others came (mostly) from the *183rd Parachute Division 'Cyclone'* and the *Arditi Distruttori of the Regia Aeronautica*.
101 The *'Ramcke'*, named after the General der Fallschirmtruppe Hermann-Bernhard Ramcke who commanded it from January to September 1943 and from June to September 1944, was created in 1943 and deployed in Italy from 26 July 1943. It took part in the occupation of Rome and the liberation of Mussolini on the Gran Sasso on 12 September 1943.
102 P. Crippa, *Storia dei Reparti Corazzati della Repubblica Sociale Italiana,* Milan, Marcia Edizioni, October 2022, p. 129, op. cit. in bibliography.
103 R. Giuseppe, *L'Organizzazione Militare della RSI: sul Finire della Seconda Guerra Mondiale*, Greco & Greco, 1998 p. 145, op. cit. in bibliography.
104 The designation of the unit in German is quoted in: N. Arena, *RSI, Forze Armate della Repubblica Sociale Italiana, La Guerra in Italia 1943*, p. 311 where it is, however, incorrectly stated as 'Spahnung Abteilung'.
105 Житомир in Ukrainian, also often transliterated as Zhytomyr or Shitomir.
106 Кіровоград, also transliterated Kirovograd.
107 P. Crippa, A. Tallillo, *Corazzati Italiani in Russia 1941-1944*, Milan, Witness to War, December 2022, op. cit. in bibliography.

The first clashes in which the armoured car drivers were wounded were at Pervomajs'k[108] against the Tatar and Mongol troops of the Red Army, who also managed to destroy the first two Armoured cars.

In one such battle that began on 20 December 1943, the *2nd Fallschirmjäger-Division* in concert with units of the *XXXXVIII. Panzerkorps* attempted to encircle several Soviet armoured and infantry units south-east of Korosten in the Meleni area. On 23 December 1943, the encirclement was not yet completed and the next day the Germans were forced to desist after the start of the Soviet Žytomyr-Berdyčiv offensive that began on 24 December 1943, retreating to Žytomyr.

On 27 December 1943, a group of 24 Arditi under the command of Capt. Paris was sent to recover three *StuG. III Ausf. G* and their crews from the *242. Sturmgeschütz-Abteilung* of the *2. Fallschirmjäger-Division* that were stuck in front of the Soviet lines. After an initial clash, the Italian arditi had to return to their own lines to replenish their ammunition and launch themselves again to attack the Soviet patrols that tried to approach the three German vehicles. In the final clash, which took place at gunpoint, the Italians managed to beat the Soviets, who left several dead and wounded on the field[109]. However, Italian losses were also heavy, with only four of the Arditi unhurt, the others being either dead or wounded. Captain Paolo Paris[110] also lost his life in the battle.

In the following days, the Soviets pressed the *2nd Fallschirmjäger-Division*, which was forced to fall back, clashing repeatedly with Red Army troops at Ol'shanka[111] (60 km west of Žytomyr), Yuzefpol and Chausovo[112].

The Dnjestr River was then crossed and further clashes took place in the villages of Duschka and Onizkan[113], where the last Armoured cars were probably lost in combat.

In February 1944, when the Armoured carers retreated west of the Prut River, they launched a final attack to break through the Soviet bridgehead that had been created on the west bank of the river and destroyed the last bridges with explosives, slowing the enemy advance[114].

The German division and the surviving armoured car drivers then concentrated in Galati, Romania and were sent to Vahn, near Cologne, where they could reorganise and rest after four months of fighting with the Soviets[115].

Despite the loss of all the *SPA-Viberti AS42 'Metropolitan' Armoured cars*, the vehicles, developed for long-range reconnaissance in desert terrain, managed to hold their own in the inhospitable Ukrainian steppes where temperatures reached just over -40° in winter. Although inadequate for the needs of the Eastern Front, where unarmoured and lightly

---

108 Первомайськ, also transliterated Perwonaisk.
109 P. Crippa, A. Tallillo, *Corazzati Italiani in Russia 1941-1944*, Milan, Witness to War, December 2022, op. cit. in bibliography.
110 Paolo Paris, born in Rome on 7 July 1915, was nominated by the RSI Minister of Defence, Marshal Rodolfo Graziani, for the Gold Medal for Military Valour, the highest decoration of the RSI, which, however, was not awarded to him due to the end of the war.
111 Ольшанка, also transliterated into Olscanka or Olshanka.
112 Unclear locations are also reported as Jusefpol and Tchaussowo.
113 C. Murray, F. Ciavattone, *Unknown Conflicts of the Second World War, Forgotten Fronts*, Abingdon on Thames, *Routledge, 1ª Edition*, September 2020, p. 200, op. cit. in bibliography.
114 C. Murray, F. Ciavattone, *Unknown Conflicts of the Second World War, Forgotten Fronts*, Abingdon on Thames, *Routledge, 1ª Edition*, September 2020, p. 201, op. cit. in bibliography.
115 Italians who lived in territories not yet liberated by the advancing Allied troops received a 40-day bonus leave for their actions during the fighting. P. Crippa, A. Tallillo, *Corazzati Italiani in Russia 1941-1944*, Milan, Witness to War, December 2022, op. cit. in bibliography.

armed Armoured cars were very vulnerable to Soviet armoured vehicles, the Armoured cars proved very useful, especially in the defence of the rear, patrolling the roads to the front. Unfortunately, the already limited Italian forces supporting the *2. Fallschirmjäger-Division* did not have enough spare parts and the last vehicles were probably abandoned due to breakdowns that could not be repaired.

In June, after the Allied landings in Operation Overlord, the *2nd Fallschirmjäger-Division* was sent to France to support the German troops in Normandy who were trying to contain the Allied forces that landed on 6 June 1944.

Remaining in Brittany, the *2nd Fallschirmjäger-Division* slowed down the Allied troops who had to clear the ports of French cities in order to receive the proper flow of supplies from England.

The bloodiest battles in which the Arditi took part took place at Carhaix (between Brest and Saint-Lò) and Landerneau (20 km east of Brest), before barricading themselves near Brest. The Arditi and the young fascists of the *Gruppo Arditi Camionettisti Italiani* fought valiantly on the side of the Germans from 7 August, the day the battle for the stronghold town began, taking part in skirmishes in the neighbouring towns of Gouesnou, Guipavas and Plouzané-Bohars[116] surrendering only on 20 September 1944. The survivors of the *Gruppo Arditi Camionettisti Italiani* ended up in a British prison camp, returning home only two years later[117].

However, the troubled history of the Arditi Camionettisti does not end in Brest. In fact, there are three different sources regarding the final fate of Italian unity:

The first is that the Arditi were captured and taken to a British prison camp near London, from which they did not return until July 1946.

The second hypothesis[118] and that the surviving Camionettisti returned home and were eventually attached to the *Italian Social Republic Parachute School in* Tradate[119] in Lombardy. Another theory reports that part of the unit escaped the Brest Sack and continued service in the ranks of the rebuilt 2. *Fallschirmjäger-Division*[120].

On 24 October 1944, the German division was recreated at Amersfoort in the Netherlands and fighting resumed against the Allied troops, but not until January 1945. The *2nd Fallschirmjäger-Division* finally surrendered in the Ruhr Sack in April 1945 and there do not appear to have been any Italians among the soldiers taken prisoner.

It is therefore possible, that a hypothetical handful of soldiers who escaped Brest actually returned to Italy in late 1944.

---

116 C. Murray, F. Ciavattone, *Unknown Conflicts of the Second World War, Forgotten Fronts*, Abingdon on Thames, *Routledge, 1ª Edition*, September 2020, p. 201, op. cit. in bibliography.
117 P. Crippa, A. Tallillo, *Corazzati Italiani in Russia 1941-1944*, Milan, Witness to War, December 2022, op. cit. in bibliography.
118 Taken from the book *Le forze armate della RSI (1943-1945), …Come il Diamante, Le Camionette del Regio Esercito* e *Gli Autoveicoli da Combattimento*.
119 The school was established on 1 December 1943 at Stroppa Castle and commanded by Lieutenant Colonel Edvino Dalmas.
120 The almost full *Fallschirm-Jäger-Regiment 6.* and the *I. Bataillon* of *Fallschirm-Jäger-Regiment 2.* managed to escape the encirclement, it is possible that among the men who were not captured there were Italians. In the book E. Finazzer and L. Carretta, *Le Camionette del Regio Esercito*, Trento, GMT, 2014, it is pointed out that some of the Italians may not have taken part in the actions in Brest because they were wounded or sick and therefore joined the *2. Fallschirmjäger-Division*, rebuilt in October 1944.

▲ A *SPA-Viberti AS42 'Metropolitana' armoured car* of the 10th Arditi Regiment surrounded by German paratroopers of the 2nd *Fallschirmjäger-Division 'Ramcke'* in Rome on 18 September 1943. It is probably a command armoured car, because it is armed only with a Breda Model 1937 medium machine gun. The picture shows the number plate 'Regio Esercito 1192B', partial camouflage above the spare wheel, the flag of the Kingdom of Italy embedded in the tread and the portrait of Benito Mussolini. (B.A.)

▲ Close-up of the driver of the *SPA-Viberti AS42 'Metropolitana' armoured car* from the previous picture: the insignia and frieze on his beret identify him as an ADRA officer. In the foreground are two German paratroopers. On the right of the Italian soldier is the Breda Model 1937 Medium Machine Gun and its mount with crank to raise the weapon during anti-aircraft fire. (B.A.)

▲ ADRA second lieutenant armed with MAB38 argues with soldiers of the 2nd *Fallschirmjäger-Division 'Ramcke'*. The officer wears the grey-green beret with the *Regia Aeronautica* frieze and the 1941 model paratrooper uniform, with Arditi flames at the lapel, over which he wears the 'samurai' corset for carrying MAB38 magazines and hand grenades. The soldiers portrayed in the picture and later ones were part of the unit of volunteers who joined the *'Ramcke'* on 18 September 1943. (B.A.)

▲ The same ADRA Second Lieutenant engaged in a discussion with some German paratroopers in the streets of Rome. Nearby one can see several vehicles with which the Italian volunteers probably reached the capital and a civilian, on the right, acting as interpreter. (B.A.)

▼ From the end of September until the beginning of October 1943, the volunteers of the *Gruppo Arditi Camionettisti Italiani* under Captain Paris, after joining the *2. Fallschirmjäger-Division 'Ramcke'*, took part in an exercise in the Albani hills with the German division and the *242. Sturmgeschütz-Abteilung*. In this picture, taken during training, one can see one of the *SPA-Viberti AS42 'Metropolitane' Armoured cars* under thick camouflage with tarpaulins and branches. (Fallaok F1675 L37 - Werner Röpke- ECPAD - Défense)

▲ The *SPA-Viberti AS42 'Metropolitana' armoured car* with the number plate 'Regio Esercito 1197B' during the same exercise, partially camouflaged with branches. On board there are Arditi wearing the grey-green uniform, while on the ground could be seen another pair of German Arditi and paratroopers. (Fallaok F1675 L37 - Werner Röpke- ECPAD - Défense)

▲ ◙ Another *SPA-Viberti AS42 'Metropolitana' armoured car* during training of the *Italian Arditi Camionettisti Group* in concert with German troops. The vehicle is missing its side ammunition box, probably lost after a violent impact that left marks on the canister racks and rear wing of the vehicle. The vehicle is equipped, like the other *Arditi Camionettisti Armoured cars*, with Pirelli 'Artiglio' type tyres. The Ardito on board is equipped with an M33 parachutist helmet. (Fallaok F1675 L37 - Werner Röpke- ECPAD - Défense)

▲ The same *SPA-Viberti AS42 'Metropolitana' camouflage armoured car* with the number plate 'Regio Esercito 1197B' (from which the acronym Eo Eto has been removed) of the *Arditi Camionettisti Italiani* at Žytomyr in Ukraine in the winter of 1943. The original camouflage is still visible under the ice and soldiers. The Arditi are all fully equipped German-style with reversible parkas and some Feldmutze. Despite the German clothing, the Arditi were allowed to use their national badges. (Nino Arena)

▲ Front view of the same armoured car. Signs of the fighting are clearly visible: one light is missing, the other is broken (visible in the previous picture), the canister rack on the right mudguard is also missing, as is the tripod for the machine gun. The armoured car retained the original Breda 20/65 Model 1935 cannon-machine gun seen in the September-October 1943 training. (Nino Arena)

▲ Another *SPA-Viberti AS42 'Metropolitana' armoured car* in service with the *Gruppo Arditi Camionettisti Italiani* assigned to the *2. Fallschirmjäger-Division 'Ramcke'*. This vehicle, also armed with a 20 mm cannon, has the number plate 'Regio Esercito 1204B' and seems to have been luckier than the other in that the battle marks left no marks on the headlights and racks. The armoured car is equipped with Pirelli 'Artiglio' type tyres and the Arditi, again wearing German type clothing. (Nino Arena)

▼ *General der Fallschirmtruppe* Hermann-Bernhard Ramcke talks with some soldiers of the *Italian Arditi Camionettisti Group*, during the campaign in the Ukraine. The German command had words of great respect for the valour demonstrated by this handful of Italian volunteers. (Nino Arena)

▲ Soldiers of the *Gruppo Arditi Camionettisti Italiani* in Ukraine in 1944 on board a *SPA-Viberti AS42 'Metropolitana' armoured car* that survived the fighting in the winter of 1943. All are wearing reversible German parkas (grey and white). (Nino Arena)

During the war period, the *Italian* soldiers of the *Arditi Camionettisti Italiani Group* had a total of 18 fallen and 26 wounded, of which 5 were repatriated due to wounds sustained in the fighting[121].

The Police Armoured cars of Italian Africa

The *Polizia dell'Africa Italiana* or PAI was a colonial police force under the *Ministry of Colonies* formed in 1936[122]. The headquarters were in Rome while the *Training School* was in the *'Pantanella' Barracks* in Via Degli Orti in Tivoli. There were also two inspectorates, in Tripoli and Addis Ababa respectively, and six African offices[123].

After the loss of the East and North African colonies, before the armistice of 8 September 1943, the *Italian African Police* units still at home were assigned public order duties in the capital. The unit in charge was the *'Cheren' Column*, about 1,300 strong[124] and equipped with 14 *AB41 armoured cars*, 12 *L6/40 tanks*, 2 *SPA-Viberti AS42 'Saharan' desert Armoured cars* and a small number of cannons and machine guns.

---

121 P. Crippa, *Storia dei Reparti Corazzati della Repubblica Sociale Italiana,* Milan, Marcia Edizioni, October 2022, p. 130, op. cit. in bibliography.
122 Initially called the Colonial Police Corps, it had a staff of 2,250 Italian officers and 6,300 Libyan, Ethiopian or Eritrean officers following the directives of Royal Decree 10 June 1937-XV, no. 1211. *'Organic Regulation of the Colonial Police Corps'*, Official Gazette of the Kingdom of Italy. 29 July 1937.
123 Tripoli, Benghazi, Asmara, Addis Ababa, Gondar and Mogadishu under 62 police battalions and 51 special units.
124 Out of a total of 1,581 PAI agents in Italy.

The *'Cheren' Column* took part in the Defence of Rome, starting firefights with the Germans as early as the evening of 8 September 1943 near the Mezzocammino military depot on the Via Ostiense and continuing almost uninterruptedly until 10 September, the day the Italian forces surrendered inside the capital. By 17:00, the time of the Italian troops' surrender, the PAI had suffered 56 casualties.

Being a police department, the *Italian Africa Police* was not disarmed by the Germans and continued its public order work even under German occupation. In the convulsive days after the clashes with the Germans, about ten Armoured cars of various types of the *Motorised Assault Battalion* were taken over, together with their crews, by the PAI so that they would not fall into German hands[125] and not to have Italian soldiers interned in prison camps. The forces taken over by the *Italian Africa Police* formed the *13ª Company* of the PAI under the command of Captain Roberto Curcio.

The vehicles of the *Italian Africa Police* were used for public order throughout the period of the German occupation of Lazio. They were portrayed on 23 March 1944 at the crossroads between Via del Tritone and Via dei Maroniti, on the occasion of the Via Rasella bombing, while they were transporting marines of the *'Barbarigo' Battalion* of the *Xª MAS Division* to the site of the massacre. Another incident involving the Armoured cars of the *Italian Africa Police* was a clash that took place on 4 June 1944 during the last hours of the occupation of the city.

To avoid capture or sabotage of the Armoured cars at the hands of the retreating Axis forces, the *13ª Company* of the *'Cheren' Column was* ordered to the Ministry of War in Via XX Settembre, to await the arrival of the Allied troops.

During the transfer, however, the armoured carettes, speeding through the streets of the city, clashed several times with the German forces. On the last stretch of road, three small Armoured cars were forced to change direction, entering Via Nazionale and opening fire with their on-board weapons at the German troops. The leading armoured car, commanded by Lieutenant Carlo Pettini of the *Italian Africa Police* with five other crew members, however, found itself in front of the American vanguards coming from Via Casilina[126].

The Americans supported by an M3 Stuart light tank, being unaware of the situation and having been alarmed by the gunfire, immediately opened fire. A 37-mm armour-piercing bullet from the US tank hit Lieutenant Pettini's *SPA-Viberti AS42 'Subway'* armoured car head-on, destroying the right frontal portion of the vehicle and killing all six crew members on impact[127].

After this unfortunate incident, the *Italian Africa Police* handed over all the vehicles in its possession to the Allies, which, at the end of the war, were handed over by the Allies to the *Public Security Guards Corps* (later to become the *State Police*). An unarmed *SPA-Viberti AS42 'Metropolitana' armoured car* was picked up in the following days by some civilians and festively carried in triumph through the streets of Rome with a giant Tricolour flag, to prevent further incidents. The surviving PAI Armoured cars together with a number of

---

125 P. Crippa, *I Reparti Corazzati del Regio Esercito e l'Armistizio, 2nd Volume*, Milan, Witness to War, op. cit. in bibliography.
126 P. Crippa, *I Reparti Corazzati del Regio Esercito e l'Armistizio, 2nd Volume*, Milan, Witness to War, op. cit. in bibliography.
127 P. Crippa, *I Reparti Corazzati del Regio Esercito e l'Armistizio, 2nd Volume*, Milan, Witness to War, op. cit. in bibliography.

▲ Two *SPA-Viberti AS42 'Metropolitane' Armoured cars* of the Italian Africa Police on 23 March 1944 at the junction of Via del Tritone and Via dei Maroniti in Rome. The vehicles are loaded with marines from the 'Barbarigo' Battalion of the X MAS Division intent on scanning the windows of the surrounding buildings after the Via Rasella bombing. The vehicles have the original Regio Esercito plates covered with new layers of paint and replaced by PAI plates fixed on the petrol can rack on the left side. The armoured car in the background is a command armoured car, without main armament and equipped with three Breda Model 1937 medium machine guns. Both vehicles are fitted with Pirelli 'Artiglio' type tyres. (Nino Arena)

▼ Lieutenant Carlo Pettini's *AS42 'Metropolitana' armoured car* from the 'Cheren' Column hit by a 37 mm bullet from the US M3 Stuart in Via Nazionale on 4 June 1944. The bullet hit the armoured car on the right side as can be seen in the picture. None of the six PAI agents on board survived. The armoured car was armed with a 20/65 Model 1935 Breda 20/65 Model 1935 Breda Medium Machine Gun and a Model 1937 Breda Medium Machine Gun and equipped with Pirelli 'Artiglio' tyres.

▲ The same armoured car driven by Lieutenant Carlo Pettini in Via Nazionale on the corner of Via Mazzarino in the days after the liberation of the capital. A crowd of curious civilians surrounds the vehicle, which is missing the spare wheel and the lid of the side ammunition box, present, however, in the first picture.

▼ A *SPA-Viberti AS42 'Metropolitana' armoured car* of the Italian African Police on the streets of Rome. The picture was probably taken in the hours after the liberation of the city or in the following days. A tricolour is placed, clearly visible, at the front to avoid incidents of friendly fire. The 'striped' camouflage pattern on the ammunition box is interesting.

▲ A *SPA-Viberti AS42 'Metropolitana' armoured car* and two L3 tanks of the *Battaglione Mobile di Pubblica Sicurezza* (Mobile Public Security Battalion) parked near the Regina Coeli prison in Rome in May 1945 during a prison uprising. The armoured car, given by the Police of Italian Africa in June 1944 to the Public Security Guards Corps, is armed with a Breda 20/65 Model 1935 cannon and three Breda Model 1937 medium machine guns. (Magazine 'Crimen')

▼ Agents of the *Battaglione Mobile di Pubblica Sicurezza* prepare to go into action to quell the prison revolt in Rome in May 1944. (Magazine 'Crimen')

▲ A *SPA-Viberti AS42 'Metropolitana'* command armoured car armed with a Breda Model 1937 Medium Machine Gun with the number plate 'Polizia 255' photographed during the same prison uprising. This vehicle and the two in the previous pictures have the classic three-tone 'Continental' camouflage, which will be replaced in the following months by the monochrome amaranth red camouflage that will remain in service with the State Police until the 1960s. (Magazine 'Crimen')

▲ Lt. Carlo Pettini assigned to the Italian Africa Police in the 13th Company of the 'Cheren' Column stationed in Rome. Pettini died on June 4, 1944 aboard the SPA-Viberti AS42 'Metropolitana' armoured car he and his crew commanded. (Courtesy of Paolo Crippa)

▲ An *AB41 Autoblinda* of the *Mobile Public Security Battalion* parked in the vicinity of Rome's Regina Coeli prison in May 1945. The autoblinda, in a peculiar camouflage scheme and with an unusual symbol painted on the turret, was most likely given by the Italian Africa Police in June 1944 to the Public Security Guards Corps along with the armoured carettes. The vehicle is equipped with Pirelli Type 'Claw' tires and has no spare tire. (Crimen magazine courtesy of Paolo Crippa)

▼ A Scotti-Isotta Fraschini 20/70 Model 1941 Cannon-Mitragliera and its crew posing for the Istituto Luce on the Greek front. (Central State Archives)

other Armoured cars and vehicles recovered after the Liberation of Rome were reused by the *Mobile Public Security Battalion* and later by the *I° Reparto Celere 'Lazio' in* Rome for several years after the war.

Transportkorps Speer and Luftwaffe

After 8 September 1943, the total number of Armoured cars used by the Germans is impossible to identify precisely.

A very limited number of *SPA-Viberti AS42 Armoured cars* were deployed by *Wehrmacht* troops on the Italian front, but very few pictures of them exist[128] and their history cannot be traced due to a lack of data. It is enough to say that their German name is not even known[129].

After October 1943, a total of 13 *SPA-Viberti AS43 Armoured cars* were produced with special specifications ordered by the German General*inspektorat der Panzertruppen* (General Inspectorate of the Armoured Forces). A delegation of German officers visited various Italian production facilities, evaluated the vehicles and armaments produced and decided whether to continue producing them for German troops.

The *SPA-Viberti AS43 Armoured carettes were* judged positively and production was confirmed by the German authorities, who also ordered a modified version.

The vehicles differed from the original ones by the addition of folding iron side rails on the sides of the wooden rear compartment.

The sides acted as backrests for the crew during the march and were lowered to increase the footprint for the servants during firing operations.

In order to fit the new tailgates, the tank supports on the rear side of the armoured car's mudguards were removed[130] and the spare wheel support was moved to the new tailgate and tilted up to 0°.

The only existing images of these German *SPA-Viberti AS43 Armoured cars* show them equipped with a *Scotti-Isotta Fraschini 20/70 Model 1939 cannon-miter*, but it seems that they were intended to be equipped with German-made 2 cm FlaK 38 automatic cannons. In fact, from the original drawing[131], racks for a total of 10 magazines of 230 rounds carried, 4 on each side and 2 at the rear, are visible on the outer sides of the sides. These racks were not present on the German *SPA-Viberti AS43 Armoured cars* equipped with Scotti-Isotta Fraschini automatic cannon.

Isotta Fraschini's weapon, developed by Alfredo Scotti, was comparable to Breda's cannon-gun in terms of range, rate of fire and power supply. The two weapons differed, however, in their internal mechanics.

It seems that all 13 SPA-Viberti *AS43 Armoured cars* modified by the Viberti workshops to

---

128 The author was able to find 3 different pictures of *AS42 'Underground' Armoured cars* in service with German troops, one was published in the book R. A. Riccio, N. Pignato, *Italian Armoured car-Mounted Artillery in Action*, Carrollton, Squadron Signal Publication, 1971, p. 27, the other two came from online auction sites.
129 After 8 September, all Italian vehicles received a German nomenclature: the *Autoblinda AB41* was the *Beute Panzerspähwagen AB41 201(i)* while, to take another example, the Tank M14/41 became the *Beute Panzerkampfwagen M14/41 736(i)*.
130 In metropolitan territory, 20-litre petrol cans were rarely carried by crews as the vehicle's range was more than sufficient.
131 Visible on p. 467 of the book *Gli Autoveicoli da Combattimento dell'Esercito Italiano (1940-1945), Tomo I, Volume Secondo*, op. cit. in bibliography.

German specifications were delivered to the *Sicherungs-Abteilungen (Motorisierte)*[132] (Motorised Protection Units) of the Transportkorps Speer[133] (Speer Transport Corps).

The *Speer Transportkorps* was a paramilitary transport organisation subordinate to the *Luftwaffe*, the *Kriegsmarine*[134], the *Wehrmacht* and the *Todt Organisation*. The latter was responsible for a wide range of engineering projects, both in Germany and in the occupied territories. The *Speer Transportkorps had the* task of escorting military convoys or convoys loaded with workers, supplies and building materials of the *Todt Organisation*[135], while providing protection for work sites and in rare cases also participating in actions against partisan troops in Italy and Yugoslavia.

The *Speer Transportkorps* was organised into Transport-Regiments divided into *Kraftwagen-Transport-Abteilungen* (Motor Vehicle Transport Battalions). *Transport-Regiment 2.* and *3.* were assigned to the *Luftwaffe* while Transport-Regiments 5. to 10. served the *Wehrmacht*[136].

In addition, there were *Ersatz-Abteilungen* (Depot Battalions), *Kraftfahr-Instandsetzungs-Regimenter* (Vehicle Repair Regiments), *Pioneer-Abteilungen* (Engineer Battalions), Nachrichten-Staffel (Signal Units), *Sanitäts-Kraftfahr-Staffel* (Medical Units) and the *Sicherungs-Abteilungen*[137].

The *Sicherungs-Abteilungen(Motorisierte) were used for* most of their service as an escort to German columns but, in the last months of the war, the armoured[138] and armed vehicles were also used in anti-partisan operations in northern Italy and the Balkans, where *Transportkorps Speer* operated in concert with other German units.

The *Fliegerabwehrkanonen Erdkampfschule Süd* (Southern Terrestrial and Anti-Aircraft Combat School) in Spilimbergo, near Udine[139] also employed a number of small Armoured cars.

The school trained antiaircraft artillery crews, perfecting antitank training with anti-aircraft guns. Its first commander was in fact Major Joseph 'Sepp' Prentl[140], who used *FlaK-Kampfgruppe* with 8.8 cm anti-aircraft guns against enemy tanks several times during his career, himself operating on at least one occasion as an artilleryman[141].

---

132 Singular *Sicherungs-Abteilung(Mot.)*.
133 Nicknamed 'Speer' after the German architect Albert Speer, Reich Minister for Armament and War Production from February 1942 to April 1945 and finally Reich Minister for Industry and Production in May 1945.
134 The *Kriegsmarine* was supplied by the *Transportflotte Speer*.
135 The *Organisation Todt* was the main customer of the *Speer Transportkorps* with a total of 40,000 out of 50,000 vehicles assigned to *Todt*'s needs, data taken from F. W. Seidler, *Das Nationalsozialistische Kraftfahrkorps und die Organisation Todt im Zweiten Weltkrieg*, München, Vierteljahrshefte für Zeitgeschichte, Year Number 32, 4th Issue, December 1984, p. 635, op. cit. in bibliography.
136 Later, *Transport-Regiment 11.* and *Transport-Regiment 11.* also joined.
137 N. Thomas, S. McCouaig, Wehrmacht Auxiliary Forces, London, Osprey Publishing, 2012, pp. 8-9, op. cit. in bibliography.
138 It seems that the *Speer Transportkorps* did not possess tanks but was nevertheless well equipped with Italian wheeled armoured vehicles, in addition to Armoured cars.
139 E. Finazzer and L. Carretta, *Le Camionette del Regio Esercito*, Trento, Gruppo Modellistico Trentino, 2014, p. 47, op. cit. in bibliography.
140 Major Prentl operated during the French Campaign, on the Eastern Front and on the Italian Front, earning five military decorations for his courage and steadfastness. For the last medal he received, the Knight's Cross with Oak Leaves, the recommendation stated that, during Operation Achse (disarming Italian troops) in September 1943, he managed to destroy or capture: 5 tanks, 6 anti-tank guns, 9 artillery pieces and imprison 1 general and 4,000 Italian soldiers.
141 During the fighting on the Eastern Front, in the Voronezh area between 24 and 25 July 1942, he destroyed a total of 18 Soviet tanks operating as the gunner of the last remaining gun of his FlaK-Kampfgruppe.

The German training school was also equipped with various other types of captured Italian vehicles, including several tanks and self-propelled vehicles that were deployed, together with its students, against the partisans in Friuli Venezia Giulia in the last months of the war[142].

Some of the *SPA-Viberti AS43 Armoured cars* captured from the Italians, or produced after the armistice, but without modifications, were instead rearmed by German *Luftwaffe* units with 2 cm FlaK 38 automatic cannons and 7.92 mm Mauser MG15 medium machine guns of aircraft origin in place of the *Breda Model 1937 medium machine guns*.

Armoured cars armed with 2 cm FlaK 38[143] of the *Luftwaffe* were deployed in the same way as the *Speer Transportkorps* Armoured cars. Mainly to escort convoys, although offensive actions against Italian partisan troops were not missing.

Another important task for the *Luftwaffe*'s armed vehicles was to patrol the areas around the military airfields to prevent coups by partisan units that, as the end of hostilities approached, attempted increasingly daring actions against the Teutonic occupiers.

The Partisan Armoured cars

Until the day of the Great Partisan Uprising on 25 April 1945, it seems that the Italian partisans had not captured any Armoured cars from the Nazi-Fascist troops.

However, an *SPA-Viberti AS42 'Metropolitana' armoured car* was used in Turin during the insurrection that began on 26 April 1945.

The armoured car is portrayed in several photographs, one of which shows it inside the *Società Piemontese Automobili* plant in Corso Ferrucci[144] topped by a group of unarmed insurgent factory workers.

The SPA plant in Turin was one of the factories to which, in early 1945, part of the production of Ansaldo-Fossati, by then on its knees after the Allied bombing, was reallocated[145].

On 18 April 1945, a general strike organised by the *National Liberation Committee* began, during which the factory workers and *Patriotic Action Squads*[146] barricaded themselves inside, blocking the secondary entrances to the factory and erecting barricades to defend themselves against Nazi-Fascist attacks[147].

At the same time, teams of workers began to organise the few resources they had available

---

142 E. Finazzer and L. Carretta, *Le Camionette del Regio Esercito*, Trento, Gruppo Modellistico Trentino, 2014, p. 48, op. cit. in bibliography.
143 The FlaK 38s had the advantage of firing the same ammunition as the Italian Scotti-Isotta-Fraschini and Breda guns (20 x 138 mm B) but with standard 30-round magazines instead of 12-round magazines like the Italian guns. The same ammunition could be chambered in Swiss-made guns (Solothurn S-18/100, S-18/1000 and S-18/1100) and Finnish-made guns (20 ITK 40 VKT and Lahti L-39).
144 The Società Piemontese Automobili, a subsidiary of FIAT, occupied a plant of 115,000 m^2 between Corso Ferrucci, Corso Peschiera, Via Osasco and Via Montenegro (today Via Paolo Braccini) and employed a total of around 5,000 workers during the war, 90% of whom took part in the uprising, but most of whom were unarmed.
145 Unfortunately, we do not have precise dates or the locations to which the production and assembly of the armoured vehicles were relocated. We can say with certainty that the Manifattura Rotondi in Novara was responsible for the final assembly of the AB series armoured cars, the Fonderia Milanese di Acciaio Vanzetti S.A. participated in the final assembly of some self-propelled vehicles in competition with the SPA in Turin.
146 The SPA teams belonged to the 4th *Garibaldi Partisan Brigade 'Leo Lanfranco'*.
147 R. Luraghi, *Il movimento operaio torinese durante la Resistenza*, Turin, Einaudi, 1958, p. 285, op. cit. in bibliography.

▲ *SPA-Viberti AS43 armoured car* of Transportkorps Speer. Neither the provenance nor the dating of the pictures is clear, but the presence of the stamp of a photographic studio on the back of the pictures suggests that they were taken in the province of Milan. In addition to being armed with a Scotti-Isotta Fraschini 20/70 Model 1939 Cannon-Mitragliera, the vehicle is equipped with a front guard to protect the crew on the front arch. The camouflage is also unusual. (Ghidoni)

▼ A Todt Organisation *SPA-Viberti AS43 armoured car* with the number plate 'OT 88751' drives along a dusty road somewhere in northern Italy. The armoured car is armed with a Scotti-Isotta Fraschini 20/70 Model 1939 Cannon-Mitragliera but has no secondary armament. On the sides are the folding iron sideboards used by the crew as a backrest. (Ghidoni)

▲ Probably the same armoured car as in the previous picture, equipped with the front armour plate roughly cut off and a steel bracket welded on to support its weight. In front of the lorry is an unrecognisable vehicle and a *Lancia Lince*, both from the *Speer Transportkorps*. (Ghidoni)

▲ An overexposed image of *SPA-Viberti AS43 Armoured cars* equipped with Scotti-Isotta Fraschini 20/70 Model 1939 guns and another gun of the same model on the ground. These are *Transportkorps Speer* vehicles probably used in a training session. (Ghidoni)

▼ A beautiful image of an *SPA-Viberti AS43* Armoured car with the modifications desired by the German occupiers. The metal side and rear rails are clearly visible as is the Scotti-Isotta Fraschini 20/70 Model 1939 Cannon-Mitragliera but there is no sign of the secondary armament. Next to the armoured car is a FIAT-SPA 38R curiously camouflaged by German Transportkorps Speer troops and armed with the same anti-aircraft weapon. (Courtesy of Paolo Crippa)

▲ Two *SPA-Viberti AS43 Armoured cars* in service with the Luftwaffe and equipped with 2 cm FlaK 38 antiaircraft guns probably during training. The armoured car in the foreground is equipped with Pirelli Type 'Claw' tires and has no secondary armament. (Courtesy of Enrico Finazzer)

▼ A second image of *SPA-Viberti AS43 Armoured cars* in service with the Luftwaffe. In this case the vehicle is armed with Mauser MG15s on the gooseneck mount. On the rear gasoline canister mount the crew placed a wooden box for extra ammunition. (Courtesy of Enrico Finazzer)

▲ A final image of *Luftwaffe* Armoured cars during training. Note the headlights fitted with covers. (Courtesy of Enrico Finazzer)

▲ A column of *Luftwaffe* vehicles probably advances into the Balkans escorted by two *SPA-Viberti AS43 Armoured cars* and a *FIAT 665NM Protected armoured car*. Both Armoured cars are without secondary armament. (Courtesy of Daniele Guglielmi via Enrico Finazzer)

▲ One of the two Armoured cars in the previous photo marching on the mountain road. The tires are Pirelli Type 'Claw' while the license plate is: 'Wehrmacht-Luftwaffe 386779,' i.e., the same armoured car as in photo number 66. (Courtesy of Daniele Guglielmi via Enrico Finazzer)

in the plant's warehouses to assemble at least three armoured vehicles[148], as well as, presumably, applying additional armour to the armoured car.

At 17:00 on 26 April 1945, an initial attack by the marines of the X^a *MAS Division*[149] was repulsed by the insurgents. The attack was followed by the cannonade of[150] by several armoured vehicles[151] of an unknown division.

Meanwhile, workers prepared to finish assembling the armoured vehicles, which were ready around 9 p.m. the same day.

However, the vehicles were useless because the workers had no ammunition for either the main weapons or the machine guns.

A few minutes after 9 p.m., a second attack was launched by the fascists who had surrounded the factory and, according to partisan reports, were equipped with two tanks, an armoured car and several Armoured cars full of squads from the I^a *Black Brigade 'Ather Capeli'*.

Just when it looked as if Sappists and workers would have to evacuate the factory to avoid being caught, an anonymous worker got behind the wheel of the self-propelled armoured car and sped out of the plant. The fascists, taken by surprise, left the battlefield without attempting any more attacks[152] on the factory.

The *SPA-Viberti AS42 'Metropolitana' armoured car*, which was probably at the SPA for repairs[153], was equipped during the occupation of the factory with armour plates on the sides of the fighting compartment and on the rear of the same to protect the occupants from enemy small arms fire. As with the armoured vehicles, it lacked armament and it is therefore likely that it was intended to be used as a support vehicle, the partisans on board would have used their personal weapons while being protected by the additional armour plating.

No data are available on the use of the armoured car in the days following the defence of the SPA. Due to its speed and transport capabilities, it was probably used for patrol duties or for rapid intervention of partisans arriving in the Piedmontese capital.

The last known appearance of the vehicle took place on 6 May 1945, when the partisan forces of Turin paraded through the city, stopping in Piazza Vittorio Veneto where they were reviewed by the president of the Piedmont *National Liberation Committee*, Franco Antonicelli, and the new mayor of Turin, Giovanni Roveda.

The vehicle was probably handed over to the Allies after the end of hostilities along with the other vehicles captured from the Nazi-Fascist forces in the city of Turin.

---

148 The 3 vehicles described seem to be 2 M15/42 Carri Armati and 1 M42M Semovente da 75/34, from G. Padovani, *La liberazione di Torino*, Milan, Sperling & Kupfer Editori, 1979, p. 166-169, op. cit. in bibliography.
149 This is a partisan claim and therefore doubtful. For certain, some marines of the X^a *MAS Division* were still present in Turin in the *'Torino' Detachment* under the command of Major Antonio Lisi with the strength, probably, of a company, with the aim of protecting the FIAT plants from attacks and looting.
150 Archivio Istituto Piemontese per la Storia della Resistenza e della Società Contemporanea, Verbali CLN Aziendali E/76/D, Fascicolo 8.
151 None of the few documents that have survived the war record the use of armoured vehicles against the SPA, but it is very likely that the armoured vehicles described were from *Armoured Group M 'Leonessa'*.
152 G. Padovani, *La liberazione di Torino (The Liberation of Turin)*, Milan, Sperling & Kupfer Editori, 1979 reports how the fascist troops thought there were other armoured vehicles inside the factory and preferred to abandon the camp rather than be overwhelmed by the partisan armoured vehicles.
153 The SPA assembled the armoured car chassis at Officine Viberti just over a kilometre away from the SPA plant, so it is unlikely that the vehicle was assembled at SPA.

▲ The *SPA-Viberti AS42 'Metropolitana' armoured car* parades through the streets of Turin with dozens of Piedmontese partisans on board during the city's liberation parade on May 6, 1945. From the covers on the headlights we can assume this was the same vehicle photographed at the SPA a few days earlier. (Piedmont Institute for the History of the Resistance courtesy of Enrico Finazzer)

▲ The same *SPA-Viberti AS42 'Metropolitana' armoured car* at the end of the parade on May 6, 1945 in Turin's Piazza Vittorio Veneto behind a 75/18 Semovente M42 and an M14/41 Tank after parading in front of the commander of the Piedmontese CLN, Franco Antonicelli, and the mayor of Turin, Giovanni Roveda. The rear and side shields of the armoured car can be appreciated in this image. (Courtesy of Daniele Guglielmi via Enrico Finazzer)

▲ *SPA-Viberti AS42 'Metropolitana' armoured car* carrying some unarmed workers from the *Società Piemontese Automobili* at 122 Corso Ferrucci in Turin. Circumstantial armor has been mounted on the armoured car, protecting the rear and part of the sides. The armoured car has 'Continental' camouflage and is adorned with the acronym "SPA" and other phrases in various places on the chassis to prevent friendly fire incidents. The side door to the front storage compartment and the cover over the spare tire are missing. Two curious details are present: covers over the headlights, and Pirelli 'Green Seal' tires for desert soils. (Piedmont Institute for the History of the Resistance)

▲ Saharan AS42 armoured car in North Africa, March 1943, crew made up of PAI elements. It was part of the '103rd Arditi Camionettisti Company', half of which fought on the Tunisian front, and the other half on the Libyan front.

▼ Camionetta SPA-Viberti AS42 'Metropolitana' utilized by two german officers

ACKNOWLEDGEMENTS

At the end of this book, we must thank all the people who made its publication possible.
My sincere thanks go to Paolo Crippa who has always been prolific with precious advice and who, first and foremost, has done his utmost to help the author, proposing the idea, reading the drafts of what is, my first book, and sharing many of the pictures.
Another special thanks goes to Enrico Finazzer for his helpfulness and to the Gruppo Modellistico Trentino, who also provided a considerable amount of images free of charge, without which we would not have been able to provide an adequate iconographic section.
No less important was the work of the friends who had the thankless task of proofreading, Daniele Notaro and Mauro Benti, whom I thank for their advice, insights and constructive criticism.
My sincere thanks also go to the publishing house staff for their work.

▲ *Camionette Sahariane AS42* in North Africa, March 1943, also PAI. engaged in a patrol in a desert area.

BIBLIOGRAPHY

- Arena Nino, *RSI, Forze Armate della Repubblica Sociale Italiana, La Guerra in Italia 1943*, Ermanno Albertelli Editore, 1999.
- Barbano Filippo, *I Fatti Militari di Alba in alcuni Documenti Partigiani e Repubblicani (10 Ottobre 1944-15 Aprile 1945)*, MLI, Numero 4, Gennaio 1950.
- Ceva Lucio e Curami Andrea, *La Meccanizzazione dell'Esercito fino al 1943, Tomo I, Parte Prima*, Roma, Stato Maggiore dell'Esercito, Ufficio Storico, 1994
- Cristini Luca Stefano, *Le forze armate della RSI 1943-1945*, Soldiershop, 2016
- Crippa Paolo, *Storia dei Reparti Corazzati della Repubblica Sociale Italiana 1943-1945*, Milano, Marvia Edizioni, Ottobre 2022
- Crippa Paolo, *I Carristi di Mussolini, Il Gruppo Corazzato "Leonessa" dalla MVSN alla RSI*, Witness to War, Maggio 2019
- Crippa Paolo, *I Reparti Corazzati del Regio Esercito e l'Armistizio, 2° Volume*, Witness to War, Maggio 2021
- Finazzer Enrico, Carretta Luigi, *Le Camionette del Regio Esercito: FIAT-SPA AS37, SPA-Viberti AS42, FIAT-SPA AS43, Desertica 43, i Reparti che le Usarono*, Trento, Gruppo Modellistico Trentino, 2014
- Guglielmi Daniele, Cioci Antonio, *I Volontari Italiani nella 2. Fallschirmjäger Division*, Storia e Battaglie, Numero 9, Settembre 2002.
- Longo Luigi Emilio, *I "Reparti Speciali" Nella Seconda Guerra Mondiale*, Milano, Mursia, 1991
- Luraghi Raimondo, *Il movimento operaio torinese durante la Resistenza*, Torino, Einaudi, 1958
- Marconi William, *L'Aprile 1945 fra Tirano e Grosio*, Tirano, Museo Etnografico Tiranese, 1996
- Murray Chris, Ciavattone Federico, *Unknown Conflicts of the Second World War, Forgotten Fronts,* Abingdon sul Tamigi, *Routledge, 1ª Edizione*, Settembre 2020
- Nava Marco, Corbatti Sergio, *…Come il Diamante, I Carristi Italiani 1943-1945*, Bruxelles, Laran Edition, 2008
- Nava Marco, *La 34^ Infanterie Division sul Fronte Italiano: 1943-1945*, Milano, Edito in Proprio, 2020
- Padovani Gigi, *La liberazione di Torino*, Milano, Sperling & Kupfer Editori, 1979, pag. 166-169.
- Patricelli Marco, *Tagliare la Corda, 9 settembre 1943 Storia di una Fuga*, Solferino, 1 Settembre 2023
- Pignato Nicola, Cappellano Filippo, *Gli Autoveicoli da Combattimento dell'Esercito Italiano (1940-1945), Tomo I, Volume Secondo*, Roma, Stato Maggiore dell'Esercito, Ufficio Storico, 2002
- Pignato Nicola, Cappellano Filippo, *Gli Autoveicoli da Combattimento dell'Esercito Italiano (1940-1945), Tomo II, Volume Primo*, Roma, Stato Maggiore dell'Esercito, Ufficio Storico, 2002
- Pignato Nicola, Cappellano Filippo, *Gli Autoveicoli da Combattimento dell'Esercito Italiano (1940-1945), Tomo II, Volume Secondo*, Roma, Stato Maggiore dell'Esercito, Ufficio Storico, 2002

- Pignato Nicola, Cappellano Filippo, *Andare Contro i Carri Armati, L'Evoluzione della Difesa Controcarro nell'Esercito Italiano dal 1918 al 1945*, Gaspari Editore, 2008
- Rocco Giuseppe, *L'Organizzazione Militare della RSI: sul Finire della Seconda Guerra Mondiale*, Greco & Greco, 1998
- Rainero H. Romain, *Il Sahara Italiano nella Seconda Guerra Mondiale*, Roma, Stato Maggiore dell'Esercito, Ufficio Storico, 2011
- Riccio A. Ralph, *Italian Tanks and Combat Vehicles of World War II*, Mattioli, Aprile 2010
- Sandri Leonardo, *Raggruppamento Anti Partigiani (RAP), Reparto Arditi Ufficiali (RAU), Una Documentazione*, Milano, Edito in Proprio, 2020
- Sandri Leonardo, *La 5^ Gebirgs Division sul Fronte Italiano 1943-1945: Una Documentazione*, Milano, Edito in Proprio, 2022
- Seidler W. Franz, *Das Nationalsozialistische Kraftfahrkorps und die Organisation Todt im Zweiten Weltkrieg*, Vierteljahrshefte für Zeitgeschichte, München, Anno Numero 32, 4° Numero, Dicembre 1984
- Technical Memorandum ORO-T-269, *Allied Supplies for Italian Partisans During World War II*, Washington DC, Department of the Army, Office of the Deputy Chief of Staff for Plans and Research, 4 Febbraio 1955
- Thomas Nigel, McCouaig Simon, *Wehrmacht Auxiliary Forces*, London, Osprey Publishing, 2012
- Thomas Franz, Wegmann Günter, *Die Eichenlaubträger 1940-1945, Band II*, Osnabrück, Biblio-Verlag, 1998

▲ *Saharan AS42 armoured car* in the version with sun shade. Note also the special masking of the front windscreen

TITOLI GIÀ PUBBLICATI - TITLES ALREADY PUBLISHING

BOOKS TO COLLECT

www.ingramcontent.com/pod-product-compliance
Lightning Source LLC
LaVergne TN
LVHW072118060526
838201LV00068B/4916